FIG TRE

and

FURNACES

For Liz and Tim
with love

FIG TREES and FURNACES

Biblical stories, scripts and reflections Esther to Maccabees

Ruth Burgess

wild goose publications

www.ionabooks.com

First published 2018 by
Wild Goose Publications
21 Carlton Court, Glasgow G5 9JP, UK,
the publishing division of the Iona Community.
Scottish Charity No. SC003794. Limited Company Reg. No. SC096243.
www.ionabooks.com

ISBN 978-1-84952-620-3

Cover photograph © Deborah Lee Rossiter | Dreamstime.com

Overseas distribution
Australia: Willow Connection Pty Ltd, Unit 4A, 3–9 Kenneth Road, Manly Vale, NSW 2093
New Zealand: Pleroma, Higginson Street, Otane 4170, Central Hawkes Bay
Canada: Bayard Distribution, 10 Lower Spadina Ave., Suite 400, Toronto, Ontario M5V 2Z

Printed by Bell & Bain, Thornliebank, Glasgow

Contents

Contents in detail

Song of Solomon

Isaiah

Jeremiah

Lamentations

Ezekiel

Daniel

Hosea

Joel

Amos

Obadiah

Jonah

Micah

Nahum

Habakkuk

Zephaniah

Haggai

Zechariah

Malachi

Tobit

Judith

The Wisdom of Solomon

Ecclesiasticus

Susanna

Bel and the Dragon

2 Maccabees

Introduction

Fig Trees and Furnaces follows on from *Olives and Obligations.*

The original intention was to publish one book of Old Testament resources. But as contributions came in it was clear that there was too much material to fit into one book. Consequently *Olives and Obligations* contains material drawn from Genesis to Nehemiah and *Fig Trees and Furnaces* contains material drawn from Esther to Maccabees.

Material from the Apocrypha is included in this collection, and it has proved to be a source of wisdom, wonder and great stories.

The First or Old Testament is a huge collection of books. Despite having read it regularly for over sixty years, in the process of putting this book together I came across characters (six-toed giants) and creatures (chameleons and snails) that I'd previously missed, and some very long names. It was fun.

The material is laid out in biblical order and consists of stories, scripts and reflections based on biblical passages. Some stories attracted more contributions than others and the collection contains both the familiar and the little known.

Thank you to all the contributors for their rich and imaginative material, which it has been a privilege to edit. Thank you, too, to the Wild Goose Publications team – Sandra Kramer, Neil Paynter, Jane Darroch-Riley and Maria O'Neill – for their professionalism and support.

As a child I sang:

God has given us a book full of stories
which was made for his people of old.
*It begins with the tale of a garden ...**

Let us read on.

* Maria Matilda Penstone

Tell me a Bible story

What kind would you like?
A love story?
A war story?
An animal story?
A story about a child?

How about Noah and the ark (and the destruction of humanity)?
Or the sacrifice of Isaac (how dare God ask this of any parent)?
Or the Psalmist dashing heads against rocks (the bit we usually leave out)?
Or the bears sent by Elisha (to tear apart impudent boys)?

There are some hideous stories in the Bible.
How do we feel about them?

Do they intrigue us?
Do they offend us?
Do they sadden us?
Do they make us ask questions?

There are some appalling stories in the Bible.
What do we do with them?

Do we tell them in Sunday school?
Do we omit them from the lectionary?
Do we try to explain them?
Do we downright refuse to read them in church?

Is it OK to pick and choose?
What's our criteria for deciding?
Do we need to read the violence along with the peace and justice?
Do we play off the Old Testament against the New?

Stories are important.
Stories are powerful.

Teach us, God, to read the Bible with wisdom and integrity.
Tell us, in the light and in the darkness, the stories we need to know.

Ruth Burgess

Esther

I said no (Esther I)

Listen to me,
women of 127 provinces,
women from everywhere.

Listen to me,
women of every tribe and time,
listen to my story.

I broke the mould.
I said no to a man.
I disobeyed my husband.

If I had not been the queen
my words and actions
would have been punished and forgotten.
I would have been silenced.

But because I was the queen
I was heard and noticed.
The king was furious.

He consulted his advisors.

His advisors decided that
they did not want me as
a role model for their wives.

I was dismissed.
A younger, more beautiful woman
was groomed to take my place.

The king sent a message to every province
stating that
husbands, in their own homes, must be respected by their wives.

Listen to me,
women of every province,

of all ages;
I send you a message too:

Women must be respected by their husbands,
in their homes and in society.

Respect and love
cannot be imposed by anyone.
They need a mutual space in which to grow.

My words and my actions
cost me my crown,
but I retained my integrity.

When you hear the story of Esther,
remember my story too.
I am Vashti.

Ruth Burgess

She wears the crown (Esther 2)

On the shoulders of Vashti,
Esther steps into the light.
She wears the crown that Vashti wore.
She knows her fears and bears the scars
that women through the ages suffered
when they stepped before a man,
and dared to say what Vashti said,
'No!'

She refused to parade her body for gawking eyes to probe,
and other queens have done the same.
And other queens have stepped before other kings,
exposing plots and revealing plans.
And other queens have not survived,
because a fresh supply of supple virgins waits in the ready room,
prepared with treatments for their seduction,

to be paraded for gawking eyes to disrobe,
to remind all women:
Do not refuse, or be replaced.

And Esther stands tall on Vashti's shoulders
with the crown pressed onto her head.
She hears the words that Mordecai proclaimed:
'Who knows? Perhaps you have come to royal dignity
for just such a time as this.'
And his words are spoken to all of us.
And her response speaks for all of us:
'I will go to the king, though it is against the law; and if I perish, I perish.'
She wears the crown of freedom now,
for she speaks words of truth
that Vashti taught her on the way,
so we would have other shoulders to stand upon,
when we are presented before other kings.

Rebeka Maples

Following Esther's example (Esther 2)

As a teenage girl looking at the Bible, it's easy to see a load of men and be immediately put off. Men in the Bible are anywhere and everywhere. You can flick to just about any page and there will be something about a man.

Finding something about a woman is a lot harder, but often it's more rewarding. Whilst some of my female Christian friends gravitate more towards Ruth, I have found a love for Esther.

As soon as I read her story, I was filled with courage. Here was a woman who was given the chance to save her people. Israel's safety was in her hands. Yes, Mordecai aided her, but it was Esther's trust, Esther's bravery, Esther's wit that saved God's people.

She took something that she had always possessed and had no control over – her beauty – and created something that came from within her. It was her reliance on God that taught her how to use her gift and, through Him, she became a heroine.

Looking at her, I can imagine she was exceptionally lonely, living in a palace where someone was plotting against her people, with a husband whom she had to have permission to go and see.

As a teenage girl with a hidden illness (one that is not obvious), it is easy to find myself isolated. It is easy to get lost in the mirror, obsessed with how I look and how I think people see me. It is easy to see myself against the world. It is easy for my courage to fail.

Following Esther's example gives me a new lease of life. She stepped into danger before she knew the way out, and relied on God to see her safely through. He didn't leave her alone – he gave her Mordecai to watch over and support her, to translate the messages she couldn't see.

Most of all, she used her gifts. Her gift was not just her beauty – that was merely the key to the palace. Her gifts were her courage and her words, and she used them boldly. God was with her. God is with me.

Kira Taylor

For such a time as this (Esther 4)

For if you keep silence at such a time as this, relief and deliverance will rise for the Jews from another quarter, but you and your father's family will perish. Who knows? Perhaps you have come to royal dignity for just such a time as this.

Esth 4:14 (RSV)

For such a time as this
we are called.
Not to keep silent
but to speak up
for the poor
for the vulnerable
for the homeless
for the hungry
for those persecuted
because of race or religion,
for those whose voices are not heard,

whose suffering goes unheeded,
whose rights are violated.

For such a time as this
we are called to take risks,
to stand alongside God's children
in Missouri,
in New York,
in the Ukraine,
in Yemen,
in Israel,
in Palestine,
in all those places
where voices are silenced
and where hatred kills.

For such a time as this
we are called
to keep the hope alive
that light shines in the darkness,
a light that cannot be extinguished,
the light of love.

The love of God with us
for such a time as this.

Liz Crumlish

Job

Once upon a time (Job 1)

Narrator: Once upon a time ... That's a phrase that lets us know we're in for a story, and in this case we're in for one of the oldest stories in the Bible. Once upon a time, there lived, in the land of Uz, a man whose name was Job.

OK, what thoughts are running around your mind? Job was an old man with a long white beard. He was the one dreadful things happened to. His so-called friends gave him dreadful advice, but eventually God sorted him out. Does the phrase 'having the patience of Job' come to mind? Enough, let's get on with the story.

Once upon a time, there lived, in the land of Uz, a man called Job. Job was a good man. He was in awe of God and turned away from evil. Job was a rich man. He owned seven thousand sheep, three thousand camels, a thousand cattle and five hundred donkeys and he had lots of servants. Job's family enjoyed each other's company. His sons and daughters often had feasts in each other's houses. Job prayed for his family and offered God sacrifices on their behalf in case any of them had unintentionally offended God.

Meanwhile, up in heaven, the heavenly beings came to meet with God, and Satan came with them. God spotted Satan and asked him,

God: Where have you come from?

Satan: I've been down on earth, walking here and there, roaming all around.

Narrator: God was interested and got into a conversation with Satan.

God: On your wanderings, have you, by any chance, seen my servant Job? There's no one on earth as good as he is. He obeys me, he's not interested in you and he turns away from evil.

Satan: Oh, I've seen him. Rich, isn't he? All those animals he owns, nice house, lots of children – you look after him well! You bless everything he does. Of course he obeys you! But take away all that he has and he'd curse you to your face.

Narrator: God thought, and then he said to Satan,

God: Let's see ... you can take away everything he has but you must not kill him. We'll see what happens.

Narrator: And Satan left God and went back to earth. Soon after this, Job was alone in his house when a messenger arrived.

First messenger: We were ploughing and the donkeys were nearby and raiders arrived from the south and stole your animals and killed your servants. Only I have escaped to tell you.

Narrator: While the first messenger was speaking, a second messenger arrived.

Second messenger: Lightning has struck all your sheep and shepherds and killed them all. Only I have escaped to tell you.

Narrator: Before the second messenger had finished speaking, a third messenger arrived.

Third messenger: Your camels have been stolen! It was raiders from the north. They killed all your servants. Only I have escaped to tell you.

Narrator: While the third messenger was speaking, a fourth messenger arrived.

Fourth messenger: There's been a storm, a dreadful storm. Your children were feasting at the home of your eldest son when a wind rose in the desert and destroyed your son's house and killed all your children. Only I have escaped to tell you.

Narrator: Then Job got up, tore his clothes, shaved his head, fell to the ground and prayed:

Job: I was born with nothing and I will die with nothing. God gave and now God has taken away. I will bless God's name.

Narrator: And that's the end of the first part of the story. What do you make of it so far?

(You may want to allow space for some discussion here.)

To be continued next week ...

Ruth Burgess, Spill the Beans

'Oh, my darling, it's you' (Job 2:10–13)

But he said to her ... 'Shall we receive the good at the hand of God, and not receive the bad?' In all this Job did not sin with his lips.

Now when Job's three friends heard of all these troubles that had come upon him, each of them set out from his home ... They met together to go and console and comfort him. When they saw him from a distance, they did not recognise him, and they raised their voices and wept aloud; they tore their robes and threw dust in the air upon their heads. They sat with him on the ground seven days and seven nights, and no one spoke a word to him, for they saw that his suffering was very great.

Job 2:10–13 (NRSV)

My parents, who are now in their 80s, had been blessed with great health until very recently, when my father began to slide into memory loss. It is a cruel process for the man who loved words, stories and jokes. He told me recently: 'I can't tell good stories any more. I can't make people laugh like I used to. I can't remember the words.' This saddens him because it was a huge part of his personality. But he's resourceful and so resorts to visual humour now and one-line quips that he can remember – it's all in the timing, as he always said.

My mother says: 'My world has become small and restricted. I know that I need to keep myself fit and active because he needs me to look after him. He would do exactly the same for me if the roles were reversed. Our options have merely become fewer but I love him.' She also said, 'We've been so happy and have had so many wonderful years and experiences together. Now we have this, and this too we will go through together.' Another way of saying perhaps, 'Shall we receive the good at the hand of God, and not receive the bad?'

The last time my parents visited me was in Ghent, where I was preaching and serving communion. As they came up to receive communion my mother ended up in one line and my father in another. I watched as his face clouded with confusion; but then, as he recognised me, temporarily a stranger in my clergy robes, his face cleared and he came to me – beaming with the joy of recognition and the words: 'Oh, my darling, it's you.' He hugged me tight and then went back to his seat.

It was one of those moments when heaven touches earth, when the world around us disappears and we glimpse the divine. For me, my father's words embodied what the Eucharist is all about: a moment of mutual recognition, relief, rejoicing, homecoming.

When Job's friends visit him they begin by doing what I believe is the main thing that needs to be done when our friends and loved ones are suffering: they recognise his suffering and weep with him; and then they sit down in the dust with him and say – nothing at all. Of course, once they start speaking and trying to find explanations for what has happened they are less comforting. But first and foremost they come just to be with their friend and to bear witness to what he is suffering. They acknowledge him as a suffering person, and by being there they show their love and support for him. My mother does this for my father. She stays with him, listens to him, brings him his pills, holds his hand, cooks his food, talks to him.

What my mother does for my father I believe all of us are called to do for one another, as a church community, as friends and fellow pilgrims. This isn't always easy but we are not alone and we should not leave one another alone either.

Ageing is something that will come to many of us and it always ends in death. I believe that this can be a good and happy ending, a homecoming, as God opens the doors of heaven to us with a beaming smile and says, 'Oh, my darling, it's you.'

Jane McBride

Good friends (Job 2:11)

Robbie, Clare and Sally were friends. They lived in the same street and they went to the same school. They were in the same class as well. Their families knew each other. Robbie lived with his dad. Clare lived with her brothers and sisters and their mum and dad. Sally lived with her sister and her mum and her granny. Robbie and Sally and Clare had known each other all their lives. Sally and Robbie had been born in the same hospital. Clare had moved to their street when she was a baby.

Clare and Sally and Robbie often played together. They liked building dens in each other's back gardens. They all liked playing games on the Xbox. They liked a lot of the same things but not all the same things. Clare liked reading stories; she often had her nose stuck in a book and didn't talk to anyone until she had finished the story. Sally liked building models and doing jigsaws. She had lots of Lego and her granny had given her a 1000 piece jigsaw for her last birthday. She did a bit of it each day. Robbie loved growing things in his garden and taking his dog for long walks.

Most of the time Sally, Clare and Robbie played happily together. They enjoyed being with each other. Sometimes they had an argument about something, but they talked to each other and worked things out between them.

For a long time Sally's granny had not been very well and now she was in hospital. One day Sally told Clare and Robbie that she didn't know if her granny was going to get better. Sally was very sad. Robbie gave Sally a big hug and Clare joined in too.

Robbie talked to his dad that night about Sally. He told his dad that he didn't know what to do to help Sally. His dad told him that giving Sally a hug had been the right thing to do. His dad said being friends was about being there to listen to people when they were sad and letting them know you cared about them.

Clare talked to her dad and mum too. She told them that she was sad about Sally's granny. She told them that she thought that Sally was going to cry and that made her want to cry. It was really hard.

A few days later Sally's granny died in hospital. Before the funeral Robbie and Clare went round to Sally's house and spent some time with her, playing with her Lego. They both gave her a hug before they went home. Sally was away from school for a week. When she came back Clare and Robbie made sure they were with her all day, in the classroom and in the playground.

Sally sometimes told Clare and Robbie stories about her granny. She told them that when she was little her granny used to read to her and sometimes took her on trips to the seaside. Her granny liked cooking and had always made her a beautiful birthday cake. There were lots of good things to remember about her granny. 'I haven't finished my jigsaw yet,' said Sally, 'and each time I put some more pieces into it, it helps me to remember my granny and I smile.'

Sally, Robbie and Clare were friends, friends that cared about each other, friends who were there for each other on good days and bad days. Sally, Robbie and Clare were good friends.

Ruth Burgess, Spill the Beans

Job's friends (Job 3, 4, 7)

You remember the story of Job?

You remember how Job had lost everything – sheep, cattle, camels, donkeys, servants, even his children. He'd lost everything and he still trusted God.

Later in the story three of Job's friends, when they heard that he was in trouble, came to visit him and be with him. His friends sat with him and listened as Job told them everything that had been happening to him. Job told them what was going on in his mind and how he was feeling. Job held nothing back. Listen to what he said:

Read Job 3:1–10. As this is a dramatic monologue, read it in whichever Bible version helps you to read it with feeling.

One of Job's friends, who was called Eliphaz, had been listening to what Job had been saying and he tried to reason with Job:

Read Job 4:1–9.

Eliphaz reminded Job that the God who they believed in looked after those who led good lives and punished those who were wicked. All the bad things that had happened to Job must mean that Job had done something very wrong and that God was angry with him.

Do you think that's how God behaves? That God dishes out rewards and punishments to us? If we are good people does God look after us? Or do you think that God is not like that at all?

Encourage people to talk with their neighbour for five minutes.

In the story, Eliphaz's argument does not work for Job. Job goes on thinking about what God is like and he tells God how he is feeling and what he is thinking.

Read some verses from Job 7:11–21.

The story of Job is not an easy story. But it gives us plenty to think about.

More next week ...

Ruth Burgess, Spill the Beans

When I see God I will recognise him (Job 14, 19)

To be read by a narrator, Job and six other voices

Narrator: So we're back with the story of Job. Job's friends had been listening to him and giving him advice, but their advice didn't seem to be helping him very much. Job had been thinking. He'd been thinking about people, about life and death, about what seems to go on forever, and what dies and disappears: big stuff. Job had been sitting looking at trees and thinking ...

Job: Trees are amazing things. You can cut them down and they sprout again. The stump of a tree can look dead, but at the first scent of water it can grow branches and bud like a young plant. Amazing. But people aren't like that. They lie down and die and nothing rouses them. They do not wake or get up again.

Narrator: You remember that Job's family had died and he was grieving. He was full of questions. Most people have questions about life and death. Different religions and different cultures develop all kinds of ideas and beliefs.

Voice 1: I think there might be something of us that goes on living when we die. Some people call it a soul. I hope there's something. But we're not going to find out until we die. Are we?

Voice 2: Maybe we come back to earth as something else. An animal maybe, or a ghost or an angel.

Voice 3: Jesus came alive again, didn't he? And he said in God's house there were lots of rooms, ready for all of us.

Voice 4: I think we die and that's it. Nothing more. Nothing.

Voice 5: Some people say if you're good you'll go to heaven, and if you're not you won't. Who knows?

Voice 6: I'm not sure about life after death, but I like to think my family and friends will remember me, so I'll live on in their memories.

Narrator: Later on in the story Job tells his friends that he knows that God cares about him. He says:

Job: I want you to remember and write down that I know that God has always been on my side and always will be. And when I see God I will recognise him.

Narrator: God, for Job, would never be a stranger.

Ruth Burgess, Spill the Beans

God asks the questions (Job 31:35–37, 38:1–11)

Have you ever been talking about something that is important to you and realised that you have said everything about it that you wanted to say? That you have explored your subject from all angles and for now you have said enough. You can sit down. This is where we find Job this week. Listen:

'Every word that I have spoken is true. Let God answer me. I will tell God everything that I have done. I will hold my head high in God's presence. The words of Job are ended.'

You may have noticed that the voice of God has been very silent during this story, but now it is time for God to speak to Job. And God speaks to Job from the middle of a storm. Close your eyes. Picture the scene. Thunder, lightning, rain, a howling wind.

God has heard Job. And now God has some questions for Job, some amazing questions:

'Who is this that questions my wisdom with ignorant empty words?
Stand up. Be courageous. And answer the questions I ask you.
Where were you when I laid the foundations of the earth?
If you know so much you can tell me all about it.
Who decided how big it would be?
Who laid out the measurements?
What kind of base was the earth laid on?
Who was chosen to lay the cornerstone?
Tell me, surely; if you were there, you will know.

Did you hear the stars singing together
or the angels in heaven shouting for joy?
Who was it who closed the gates to hold back the sea?
Who made the boundaries?
Who said to the sea: "You must stop here and come no further"?
Job, have you ever, in all your life, commanded a day to dawn?'

You might want to read more of God's questions to Job in chapters 38, 39 and 40 of this story. It is beautiful poetic writing. The words and questions and ideas put into God's mouth are stunning, even now in the twenty-first century.

God and the universe are huge. We know so much, and yet there is so much more we have to learn.

There will always be mystery. We will always be full of questions.

Ruth Burgess, Spill the Beans

Wonderful world (Job 38)

Seren loved looking at the stars. When she was very little she could remember her mum wrapping her up in a blanket and carrying her outside and pointing to the different stars and telling her their names. Now that she was nine she could recognise some of the stars and constellations and planets on her own. There was Cassiopeia that looked like a big W, and the Plough that looked like a big saucepan. And she knew where to look for Orion with the three stars in his belt. Seren knew that her mum and dad loved looking at the stars, too. Maybe that was why they had called her Seren. It's the Welsh word for 'star'.

Seren lived in the town, so sometimes the streetlights made it hard to see the stars, but this year her mum and dad were taking her on holiday to the country and they hoped that there everything in the night sky could be seen more clearly.

Alexander loved the sea. He lived near it. He could hear the waves when he opened his bedroom windows. He liked walking on the beach doing something called beachcombing. This meant looking along the tideline to see what had been washed up by the tide – all kinds of things – sometimes a jellyfish or an egg case from a shark, which was called a mermaid's purse. Sometimes an orange soaked in the salt water. And nearly always seaweed. Lots of seaweed.

Sometimes in the summer Alexander and his mum went snorkelling. That is swimming in the sea wearing a mask so that you can see what is in the sea beneath you. He had seen lots of different fish and he knew that if his shadow fell over a crab the crab would bury itself in the sand. Alexander had seen television programmes filmed underwater in the sea. He hoped that when he was older he would be able to dive deep under the water and go exploring to see what he could find.

Do you like looking at the stars, or swimming in the sea, or travelling to different places? What questions do you have about the world in which we live?

We know lots of things about the earth and the seas and the skies but scientists are always finding out about new things. We live in a wonderful world.

Ruth Burgess

A world of answers (Job 38, 41, 42)

So, what if there was an answer for everything?
What if it all made sense?
What if everything could be explained?
What if everything could be understood?
What if there were no mysteries?
Nothing unresolved.
Nothing lacking closure.
Nothing left hanging.
Nothing to puzzle over.
Nothing beyond our control.
What if every 'why' had a clear 'because'?
What if there was an end to wondering?
What if all matters could be settled?
What if all lines of enquiry returned all necessary evidence?
What if we could get it all covered?
All worked out.

All neat and tidy.
No ragged edges.
No unfinished business.
What if we could find a place for everything
and put everything in its place?
No anomalies.
No contradictions.
No paradoxes.
No ambiguities.
What if every single question could be answered?
What if all fears could be tamed,
all monsters turned into pets,
and the rain never again fell on wasteland
or watered the wilderness?
What if we had that world?
Would we want it?

Jo Love, Spill the Beans

Questions with no answers (Job 38, 41, 42)

'I like asking questions!' said Luke to his friends one day.

'Me too!' said Penny. 'I like asking questions that nobody can answer!'

'Sometimes if I have a big question, I ask my mum,' said Luke, 'and I'll say: "But why, mum? Why?" And sometimes she says, "Just because." And I say, "But that's not an answer, mum!"'

Penny and the others all giggled. They had all heard people say, 'Just because!' when you tried to ask why.

'It means they don't know the answer!' laughed Paul.

'Let's think of all the questions we've tried to ask that nobody could answer,' said Luke.

That got everyone thinking. Here are some of the questions Luke and his friends had asked that nobody could answer:

When birds stop flapping their wings, why do they not fall out of the sky?

Why does the sky never run out of rain?

Why can you sometimes see the moon in daytime? And why can you never see the sun at night?

Why can't doctors make everyone who gets ill get better?

What is there at the edges of outer space?

When we die, will we meet people who died before us?

Who made God?

Are there some things that happen that are just pointless and meaningless?

How come no two people are exactly the same?

- *What questions would you add?*
- *How do you think you would feel if every question you asked could be answered?*
- *How do you feel about there being some things we'll never know and never quite understand?*
- *What is your favourite mysterious thing about the world?*

Jo Love, Spill the Beans

Where were you? (Job 38)

Where were you when I gave birth to the universe; when my Wisdom called forth particles from the womb of the cosmic void and seeded them into the realm of existence?

Who marked off its dimensions and form and let matter prevail over anti-matter?

On what were its footings set or who provoked its mighty expansion in the blinking of an eye?

How deeply do you comprehend the gift of light or understand the mysteries of its nature?

Who of you knows from where the sounds that fill the cosmos emanated or how music distilled its harmonies from the roaring cadences of creation?

Who gave water its extraordinary properties, decreed its many forms and accorded roles to each that it might adhere to the surfaces of gathering spheres, to nurture and give shape to barren terrains?

Can you make sense of the patterns of constellations as they would be seen from planets in the extreme reaches of the universe?

Can you leap between galaxies or refashion the orbits of stars or planets, or yet fully understand the fundamental forces of the cosmos?

Can you yet contemplate travelling to the beautiful Pleiades or loosening the cords of Orion?

Have you fully uncovered the laws of the universe or can you emulate God's care for it?

Could you reduce turbulences that beset distant planets, weather the extreme storms on other worlds or alter the path of the arrow of time?

Have you even perfected knowledge of your own benign planet, understood the reason for its existence and how to encourage your own people to act as responsible stewards of it?

Can you fathom in your exquisitely fashioned brain the mind of your Maker or conceive the depth of his love?

Will you ever understand enough to render praise and thanksgiving truly worthy of the Creator of heaven and the entire cosmos?

Trevor Thorn

No longer the same (Job 42)

Something has changed. What am I saying? Everything's changed! When you lose it all: the people you held dear, the possessions you treasured, the health you took for granted, you lose it forever.

So his body is well again. His wealth is restored. His family has grown. But that does not bring back the past. That does not mean life is the same as it was, normality has returned. Far from it.

You would think people would be talking about how doubly blessed he is these days. More head of cattle and sheep than ever before. More camels and donkeys than anyone who has ever lived. Yes, he seems happy again, rejoicing even.

But that is not the most surprising thing.

He has been throwing great feasts for his brothers and sisters and they have all brought him silver and gold and their sympathy and comfort for all he endured.

But that is not the gossip that is going round.

No, what has set the neighbourhood buzzing are his new inheritance plans. The man who came so close to death has changed his mind about who will receive a portion of his estate.

He has instructed equal shares be given to his daughters – equal to his sons! Why would he do that?

And to make no mistake, they are named – those names he chose for the beauty he sees in them: Jemima, the Dove; Keziah, the Sweet-scented oil; Keren-Happuch, the Radiant Eye.

Something's changed. He's not the same person. How could he be? But of all the ways to be affected by his ordeals, this is the strangest – giving his daughters an inheritance. Why? What is he trying to say? After all his complaints that God cannot be fathomed!

Jo Love, Spill the Beans

PSALMS

I sleep in peace (Psalm 4)

You have given me joy.
You have shown me kindness.

You hear me when I pray.
You help me when I'm in trouble.

I think about you at night.
I feel you breathe in the silence.

When I sleep, I sleep in peace.
You bless me and keep me safe.

You have put joy in my heart.
I put my trust in you.

Ruth Burgess

In early mornings (Psalm 8)

On the lips of children and of babes you have found praise
(Ps 8:2a, Grail translation)

In early morning's
'goo-goos',
we hear your
glory sung;

in evening's
lullabies full
of 'ba-bas',
we are cradled
in your
grace.

Thom M Shuman

How long, God? (Psalm 13)

For two voices or groups of voices

How long?
How long, God?
It feels like you've forgotten me.
Will it feel like this forever?
How long will you refuse to look at me?
How long must I suffer?
How long must I be so sad?
How long will those who hate me laugh in my face?
How long, God?
How long?

(Interval of music: verse 1 and 2 of 'How long, O Lord', by John L Bell and Graham Maule, from When Grief Is Raw, *Wild Goose Publications)*

Please, God, hear me.
Give me light in my darkness.
Please, God, answer me.
I don't want to die.
Can't you hear my enemies rejoicing?
They rejoice because I'm hurting.
Please, God, hear me.
Please, God, answer me.

(Interval of music: verse 3 of 'How long, O Lord')

I trust you, God, I trust you.
I trust in your strong love.
I know that you care about me.
I know that you will save me.
I will sing to you, God, I will sing.
I will sing of your strong love.
You will always be kind to me.
You will always love me.

Ruth Burgess, Spill the Beans

How long? (Psalm 13)

Michael was fed up. His friend Joseph was supposed to have been coming round to his house to play at 2 o'clock, and it was now 3 o'clock, and Joseph hadn't turned up. Michael had tried texting Joseph but there was no answer.

How long is he going to be? thought Michael. How long? ...

Max and Ailsa were on their way to see their granny. It was a long journey and they'd been in the car for ages. Max had a look at the map to see if he could work out how far they had to go. It looked like they were more than halfway there.

They had been travelling quite quickly – but now the car was going very slowly. 'What's happening, mum?' said Ailsa. 'Why are we going so slowly?'

'There's a big lorry up ahead,' said her mum, 'and it's slowed all the traffic down.'

'How long is it going to take to get to granny's?' said Max. 'How long, mum? How long? ...'

Clare was cross. She and her friend Pete had just come back from the funfair. One of the rides that Clare and Pete had wanted to go on had a measuring stick by the ride entrance. If you were as tall as the stick, or taller, you could go on the ride; if you were shorter than the stick you weren't allowed on. Clare and Pete were in the same class at school and Clare was two weeks older than Pete, but she was an inch shorter. Pete was allowed on the ride and Clare wasn't.

Pete was a kind boy and a good friend and he told Clare that if she couldn't go on the ride, he wouldn't go on either. He would wait.

How long will it be until I grow an inch? thought Clare. How long will we have to wait until I can go on the ride with Pete? How long? ...

Surrinder had chickenpox. It was horrible. Her spots were itchy and her throat was sore. She felt hot and sticky. Her eyes ached if she tried to read. She couldn't see her friends in case they got chickenpox too. She couldn't even go downstairs and watch the television. Her mum and the doctor said that she had to stay in bed. Surrinder was sad.

How long will it be before I'm better? Surrinder wondered. How long? ...

Ruth Burgess, Spill the Beans

God's glory (Psalm 19:1–6)

A: The sky shows us God's glory.
It shows us what God has made.

B: The sun comes out in the morning
like a bride and bridegroom full of joy.

A: The sun comes out in the morning
like an athlete eager to run a race.

B: The sun starts at one end of the sky
and moves across to the other.

A: The sun is full of light,
nothing can hide from its heat.

B: Without words, the sky speaks of God's glory.
It shows us what God has made.

Ruth Burgess

God tells us how to behave (Psalm 19:7–11,14)

A: God tells us how to behave.

B: God shows us what is right.

A: God teaches us to be fair.

B: God gives us wisdom and strength.

A: God's truth is more precious than gold.

B: God's wisdom is sweeter than honey.

**All: May our thoughts and words make God smile.
May our actions make God happy.**

Ruth Burgess

I'm alive today (Psalm 23)

I'm alive today.
The care of God will guide me.
God is strong and he can lift me up.
The strongness of God will look after me.
God is wise and he can teach me.
God can tell me what to say.
God shows me the way of life.
God tells me when my enemies are here.
God is looking, God is listening all the time.
God knows the way I am going: he tells me when I'm bad.
God watches over me and God listens to me.
Holy Spirit be in my speaking.
You hear me everywhere on earth from heaven.
Help me from getting into trouble.

A class of seven-year-olds reflecting on Psalm 23

The Lord is … (Psalm 23)

David, either pacing or at table with pen in hand:

The Lord is my …
The Lord is my … dustman?
I shall not want.
He picks up my litter
and empties my rubbish away.
No. That's not quite right.

The Lord is my …
The Lord is my … firefighter?
I shall not want.
He pours forth water
and extinguishes my flames.
No. That's not right either.

The Lord is my …
The Lord is my … mechanic?
I shall not want.
He fixes my squeaky wheels
and leads me to quiet motoring.
No. Still not quite there.

The Lord is my …
The Lord is my … farmer?
I shall not want.
He ploughs the green meadows
and harvests the golden fields.
Hmm. Better.

The Lord is my …
The Lord is my … goatherd?
I shall not want.
He makes me to chew anything I find
and ties me up behind the barn.
Oh, I thought I had it. But I am close.

The Lord is my …
The Lord is my … shepherd!
This could work.
The Lord is my shepherd.
I shall not want.
He makes me to lie down in green pastures;
he leads me beside the still waters.
He restores my soul …

That's the one!

Spill the Beans

The entire cosmos (Psalm 24)

The entire cosmos is the Lord's and everything in it: every particle of matter both observable and hidden, the earth's resources and living creatures entrusted to humans, and living beings of planets far beyond our reach.

Who shall travel beyond, into the eternal presence of the Lord, or who shall dare to approach that holy place? Those who have clean hands and pure hearts, who love righteousness and godly justice, who hate greed and iniquity: they will receive blessings from the Lord and be welcomed into his kingdom of love.

This can become a renewed generation of those who revere God, who stand in awe at the unfolding of the magnificence of his creation.

Lift up your heads, you galaxies; and make a dazzling pathway, you nebulae, that the King of Glory may pass among you.

Who is this King of Glory? It is the Lord, the mighty Creator whose Word brought forth this nurturing universe.

Lift up your heads, you galaxies; and make a dazzling pathway, you nebulae, that the King of Glory may pass among you.

Who is this King of Glory? It is the Lord, the Almighty, our compassionate Creator, Redeemer and Great Sustainer.

Trevor Thorn

I'm not afraid (Psalm 27:1–6)

I hear they're out to get me.
They want to pull me down and they want me to know it.
Hate is a strong word, but not too strong a word for this.
I can't believe it has escalated so fast.
One disagreement, one difference of opinion
and the whole situation spirals out of control.
But I'm not afraid.
God knows the truth and that's the light I'll walk by.
What more could they do to me?
They could still make things a lot worse.
They could stir up all kinds of lies
and paint me as the real enemy.
Yes, it hurts.
It hurts when people you thought had more sense
are actually taken in by the vicious rumours.
I've never felt so aware of the power of evil –
there is no other word for it.
Could any of them take it further?
Is my life in danger as I walk the streets?
Should I stay behind closed doors, out of sight?
What if there's someone angry enough,
vengeful enough, to attack me?
What would I want to do to someone
if I believed what they believe about me?
But do I really have need to fear?
God is my strength and what a strength that is!
I will live my life as I always have.
Let them do their worst.
Let them plan my ultimate downfall.
The criminal record will be theirs, not mine.
The only place I'm going to hide
is in the shadow of God's presence.
I won't be cowering there – no, I will be singing!

Jo Love, Spill the Beans

I'm going to be OK (Psalm 27:1–6)

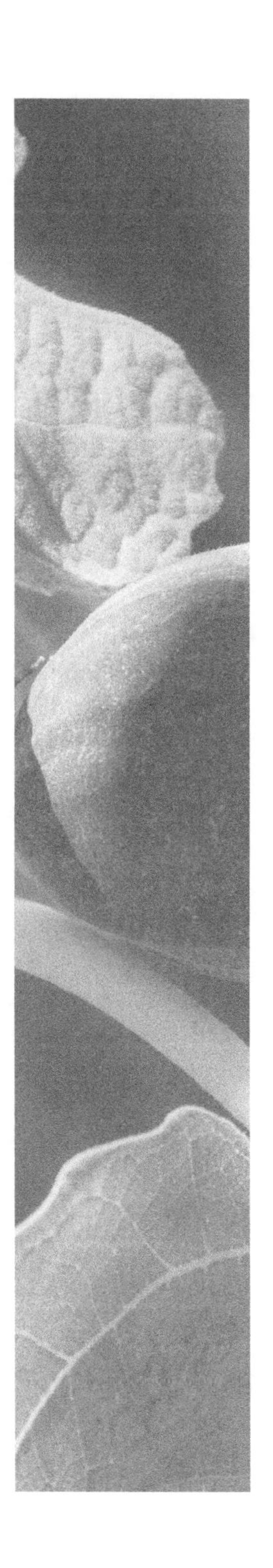

God is like a light for me.
I am not afraid!
God is looking after me:
I'm going to be OK!

If anyone is bad to me,
God will still be near.
If people try to hurt me,
God will still be here.

God is like a light for me.
I am not afraid!
God is looking after me:
I'm going to be OK!

When everyone's against me,
when everything goes wrong,
God keeps on loving me,
and so I'll sing this song.

God is like a light for me.
I am not afraid!
God is looking after me:
I'm going to be OK!

God is like a hidey-hole!
God is like a rock!
God is watching over me
'round and 'round the clock!

God is like a light for me.
I am not afraid!
God is looking after me:
I'm going to be OK!

Jo Love, Spill the Beans

Keep me from falling (Psalm 28:1)

To you, O Lord, I call; my rock, do not refuse to hear me, for if you are silent to me, I shall be like those who go down to the pit. (Ps 28:1, NRSV)

Just a
word:
of grace,
or hope;
maybe love,
or even
reprimand,
can keep me
from
falling into that
mess
where I can
never find my
way out (on
my own).

Thom M Shuman

God's voice is like thunder (Psalm 29)

God's voice is like thunder –
like a big booming drum!

God's voice is like
the rushing of a waterfall!

God's voice is like
the flashing of lightning!

God's voice is like the sound
of a huge tree trunk cracking!

God's voice is like the wind
whistling through leafy branches!

When God has something to say,
the earth shivers and shakes!

When God speaks,
he gives us strength and peace!

What do you think God's voice is like?

John Murning, Spill the Beans

You have set my feet at large (Psalm 31:8)

Feet at large,
tramp over broken pavements,
walk up hospital stairs,
squelch noisily on raw mud,
stride over furrowed soil,
step slowly through fine sand.

Feet at large,
move freely in today's wind,
leave prints in the amber dune,
torn and blown,
transient, but telling their tale;

a story of many miles,
a story of hills, dark
caves and lit valleys,
cracked edges,
challenging slopes.

You set my feet at large,
shod in boots or sandals,
walking in sunshine or snow.

Judy Dinnen

I waited and you did it (Psalm 40:1–11)

I waited and you did it, God.
You heard my cry.
You grabbed me and pulled me out of the quicksand.
You put my feet on rock.

There's no one like you, God, no one.
When we trust you we're happy.
You've done amazing things –
amazing –
and you've got great plans for us,
more plans than we can ever imagine.

You don't want sacrifices, God.
You don't want us offering you presents to make things right.
You want us to listen,
to hear and read what you are saying to us.
You want us to live by your standards
in everything we do.

I love you, God.
I want your words inside me,
in my mind
and on my heart.

I have talked about you, God.
I have told my story.
I wasn't silent, God.
I stood up in front of everyone and told them
how much you helped me.
I spoke of your justice and how faithful you are.
I told them about your steadfast love.

I know, God, that your love will always keep me safe.

Ruth Burgess, Spill the Beans

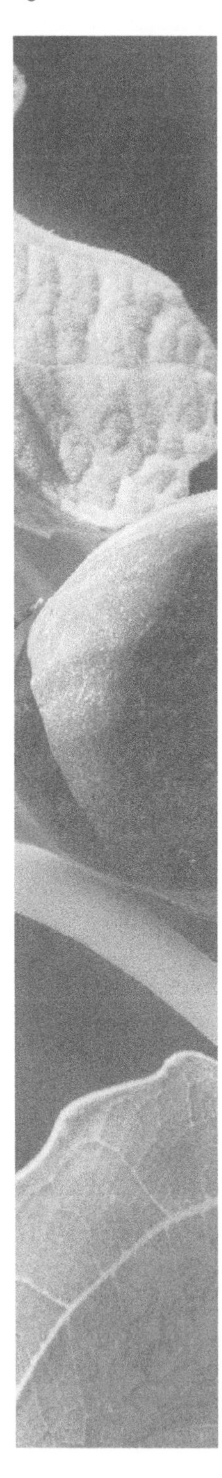

Deep calls to deep (Psalm 42:7)

It was an offer we extended to all the family – as so many grandparents do. We thought about it carefully, then waited for an appropriate gathering of the whole gang and announced: 'We are getting old and will soon leave our home of many years. We want each of you grandchildren to choose some things to remind you of life with us.'

They stared at us for a moment, pondering this strange invitation. We could see them thinking through the meaning of what they had just heard. But, after questions, hugs, consoling grins and sighs – they took us at our word.

Finally, the respectful question came back to us: 'What should we pick?' So, the walk began – all around our old house. What fun for my wife and me! I am known as 'PopPop', the patriarch of this gang of grandchildren. And soon PopPop and Gran were happily explaining the connections and personal history that oozes from every picture, pot and table – the tapestry of memories that drapes our home.

As the tales flowed, their pencils moved, making lists that included antique pictures where no one smiles back, a page from a 1611 Bible, Civil War bullet castings, pie-top and drop-leaf tables, rope beds – and even modern art. Clearly, they were excited by all of these offerings. We assured them that no request was out of bounds.

That is when our 9-year-old grandson surprised us. He said: 'I want PopPop's ashes. That's my first choice. That way, I can always have him close and talk with him.'

Nervous chuckles erupted from the others – uncertain what to say – and then gentle teasing and flat-out joking about how and where my ashes should, one day, be stored.

Soon I could see that my grandson needed a hug to reassure him that his sincere request wasn't being dismissed. I whispered in his ear: 'I like your choice.'

I heard his choice as he meant it: I don't want to be without him; he doesn't want to be without me. As in families around the world, we had cared for each other, laughed with each other and shared stories, comforted each other when sick. We had giggled, danced, read, laughed, played, wrestled, snuggled, talked about God and girls. He knows my love. I know his love. And so this request: 'I want PopPop's ashes.'

Across the generations, his deep was calling to my deep.

Benjamin Pratt

God is our shelter (Psalm 46)

All: **God is our shelter, our safe home.**
God helps us when we are in trouble.

A: When things around us change
we need not be afraid.

B: God is where we live,
in our village, our city, our town.

A: God is stronger than fighting and wars.
God is stronger than winds and storms.

B: Be still and know God's peace inside you.
Be still and know God's love.

All: **God is always with us.**
God is our shelter and our safe home.

Ruth Burgess

Like a green olive tree (Psalm 52:8–9, Psalm 92:12–15)

I am like a green olive tree
growing in God's house:
I flourish.

I put my trust
in God's love and mercy:
I grow.

In the presence of friends and strangers
I tell of God's goodness:
I shout.

Planted in God's house
honest people are nourished:
they blossom.

Even in old age
they are green and vigorous:
they fruit.

Their lives affirm God's goodness;
God is their strength:
they live.

Ruth Burgess

With all creation (Psalm 65)

In all creation we see you, God,
in earth and sea and sky. In mountains
standing tall and mighty we see
your strength and we find courage.
In roaring seas made calm and still we see you,
powerful, and we hear you
in the silence.
In places far

and out of reach to humans you are seen
with awe and wonder. In every dawning
of the day and each falling of the night,
the sky delights to show your beauty,
shimmering golden gateways to joy.

In the emptying clouds, we feel your touch,
and with the grains and flowers stretch towards
your gift of life. In water falling, tumbling,
washing, rough edges grow smooth and we see,
if we are patient, your patient, constant
presence. In growing and in reaping, in
dying and in planting, we see a richness to this
life with you; we dance with birds and sing
the music of the hills and valleys – together
will we sing, inhabitants of earth, in joy
and in thanksgiving, in praise of Holy God.

Sarah Agnew

Three score years and ten (Psalm 90)

Three score years and ten ...

A moment in time to you, God,
you who breathed life into me
at my beginning,
you who are my home.

I gave blood
on my seventieth birthday, God;
it felt good to still be able to give life,
to share it.

*Four score years, if we are strong,
and then we fly away.*

I am old,
old becoming, hopefully, wise.

Teach me how to number my nights and days.

Finish off what you began in me
seventy years and nine months ago.

Finish it well.

Ruth Burgess

When you're in trouble (Psalm 91:15)

This is what God says:
I will be with you when you're in trouble.

When times are hard,
when things go wrong:
I will be with you when you're in trouble.

When you make mistakes,
when you feel ashamed:
I will be with you when you're in trouble.

I will hear your prayers.
I will stand by you.
I will be with you when you're in trouble.

Ruth Burgess, Spill the Beans

In old age (Psalm 92:14)

In old age they still produce fruit; they are always green and full of sap. (Ps 92:14, NRSV)

Parkinsoned hands
can still help
build homes for others;
dimmed eyes
can tell story after
story to little kids;

weakened voices
are able to
cry out for justice;
fading ears
listen to the
whispers of hope,
if we would just
stop writing the formula:
ageing = useless.

Thom M Shuman

A joyful noise (Psalm 100)

For 5 voices and a narrator

Narrator:	Make a joyful noise to God, all the earth.
Voice 1:	Blackbirds sing.
Voice 2:	Leaves rustle.
Voice 3:	Volcanos rumble.
Voice 4:	Bees buzz.
Voice 5:	Drums roll.
Narrator:	Worship God with gladness; come into God's presence with singing.
Voice 1:	Morning has broken.
Voice 2:	If you're happy and you know it ...
Voice 3:	All you need is love.
Voice 4:	The hills are alight.
Voice 5:	All things bright and beautiful ...
Narrator:	Know that God made us and to God we belong. We are God's people. We are the sheep and God is our shepherd.
Voice 1:	God loves us and made us to love each other.

Voice 2: We are God's family.
Voice 3: God is our shepherd.
Voice 4: Baaaaaaaaaaa ...
Voice 5: Maaaaaaaaaaa ...

Narrator: Enter God's gates saying thank you;
come into God's house and be glad.

Voice 1: We are welcome.
Voice 2: We are at home here.
Voice 3: We are happy here.
Voice 4: We are family.
Voice 5: We belong.

Narrator: God is good;
God's love goes on for ever and ever.

Voice 1: God loves our grandparents and our parents.
Voice 2: God loves our brothers and sisters and aunties and uncles and cousins and foster parents and guardians.
Voice 3: God loves our friends and our enemies.
Voice 4: God loves our children and our grandchildren.
Voice 5: God loves us all.

Voice 1: For ever
Voice 2: and ever
Voice 3: and ever
Voice 4: and ever
Voice 5: and ever
All five voices
& narrator: Amen

Ruth Burgess, Spill the Beans

Dartmoor psalm

Adapted from Psalm 104

Praise the Lord, O my soul.
O Lord my God, you are very great;
he set the earth on its foundations
and clothed it with the waters.

He established the uplands and the valleys
making grass to grow for the cattle.
He makes plants to blossom and fruit –
bringing forth food even from the high places.

Spring water that refreshes our bodies,
meat to give us strength and whortleberries that bring us joy.
The trees of the Lord are well-watered,
the rowans and hawthorns he tends.

On the moor, birds make their nests;
the heron has its home in the pine trees.
The high tors belong to the ring ouzel;
the crags are a refuge for the ponies.

The moon marks off the seasons,
and the sun knows when to go down.
Darkness grows into night,
and the owls glide over the moor.

The foxes hunt for their prey
and seek their food from God.
The sun rises, and they steal away;
they return and lie down in their dens.

People go out to their work,
to their labour until evening.
How many are your works, O Lord!
In wisdom you made your creatures.

These all look to you
to give them their food at the proper time.
When you open your hand,
they are satisfied with good things.

When you hide your face, they are terrified;
when you take away their breath, they die and return to the dust.
When you send your Spirit, they are created.
You renew the face of the earth.

May the glory of the Lord endure forever;
may the Lord rejoice in his works –
I will sing to the Lord all my life;
I will sing praise to my God as long as I live.

Note: Not much that can be eaten grows on Dartmoor – certainly not vines to make wine or wheat to make bread! Whortleberries are a local name for bilberries. 'Tor' is a term for a hill or rocky peak and is a much-loved feature of this Devon moor.

Simon Taylor

God, you are big and strong (Psalm 104)

A: God, you are big and strong.
You are beautiful and full of light.

B: You use the clouds as your chariot.
You ride on the wings of the wind.

A: You made the earth with its mountains.
You spread out the seas like a velvet cloak.

B: The trees get plenty of rain
and in them the birds build their nests.

A: Lions roar in the darkness.
Badgers hide in the cliffs.

B: Sea monsters play in the oceans
and ships sail on the seas.

A: God, you have created so many things.
May you be happy with what you have made.

**All: We will always sing songs to God.
May God enjoy our songs.**

Ruth Burgess

A monster (Psalm 104:26)

'Leviathan is there – that sea monster you made to amuse you.' (Ps 104:26, GNB)

You made a monster, God.
A sea monster to have fun with,
a sea monster to be your friend.

Wow!

I wondered what your monster looked like
and Google found me the Book of Job.

Your monster is huge!
Light flashes when he sneezes
and his eyes glow like the rising sun.
His back is hard and spiky
and he can dive and swim.

He churns up the sea like boiling water;
he makes the oceans bubble and dance.

What a monster, God.
He sounds amazing.
Did you play tag with him?
Did you both sing with the selkies?
Did you dive with him under fishing boats and ships?

Did he have superpowers, your monster?
Could he make himself invisible?
Could he live for thousands of years?

I wonder, God, what it would be like
to be able to create a monster to play with –
an enormous living monster,
a monster to be my friend.

Ruth Burgess, Spill the Beans

The beginning of wisdom (Psalm 111)

If I were sent into exile with only one book, I would probably choose the Psalms, in which I find comfort, wisdom, poetry and song. Like various other elderly persons, I do insist, though, that if the King James version was good enough for St Paul then, where the Psalms are concerned, it's good enough for me. Modern translations and paraphrases of the Psalms are a cultural outrage to my mind.

Some of the Psalms are horrific if left in the wrong hands – take Psalm 137, for example. I need expert help with 'Happy shall he be that taketh and dasheth thy little ones against the stones.' And then there was a verse from Psalm 121, heard at a funeral recently: 'The sun shall not smite thee by day.' After dealing with skin cancer I was ready to jump up and call the minister on that one. But working back a little more, we come to a favourite, Psalm 111 and 'The fear of the Lord is the beginning of wisdom.' That was Bishop William Elphinstone's motto for his newly founded university in Aberdeen in 1495, and it left an impression on me from the day I arrived there half a century ago. I am not a notably pious person – you don't meet a lot of notably pious engineers – but there is something fundamental about that phrase that resonates; perhaps because it has an enduring ring of truth to it.

Andrew Foster

They rise in the darkness (Psalm 112)

They rise in the darkness as a light for the upright; they are gracious, merciful and righteous. (Ps 112:4, NRSV)

We long to stay
in bed, cosy
and warm
under the covers
of our apathy
and doubts, but
you splash
cold water on our faces,

throwing clothes at us,
inviting us to join you in
feeding the hungry,
sheltering the poor,
warming the cold
who are standing out
in the pre-dawn shadows.

Thom M Shuman

From where will my help come? (Psalm 121:1)

I lift up my eyes to the hills – from where will my help come?
(Ps 121:1, NRSV)

You shaped the
stars,
yet thought
to put a
twinkle
in our
eyes;

you carved
rivers
through canyons,
and gave us
tears to
share with
laughter;

you shattered
moons
into asteroids,
and put
hearts

deep within
us which break
for others;

you ignited that
spark
which flung
universes
into space, yet
lovingly
take a
moment to
help us.

Thom M Shuman

Where does our help come from? (Psalm 121)

A: Where does our help come from?

B: It comes from God who made heaven and earth.

A: God doesn't go to sleep and forget us.

B: God is always awake.

A: God loves us and looks after us.

B: God guards us day and night.

A: When we go out God is with us.

B: When we come home God is by our side.

**All: God is always with us.
For ever and ever and ever.**

Ruth Burgess

You pick the lock (Psalm 124:7)

We have escaped like a bird from the snare of the fowlers;
the snare is broken, and we have escaped. (Ps 124:7, NRSV)

You pick the lock
on the cage
where we are trapped
by our old friend death,
and gently reaching
in,

you pull us out
and whisper,
'Fly, fly!'
releasing us into the
Spirit's breeze.

Thom M Shuman

The checklist (Psalm 127:1)

Unless the Lord build the house, its builders labour in vain. (Ps 127:1)

Scene: A committee meeting to discuss proposals for a new church development project. Members are seated around a table. The secretary is standing nearby (or alternatively sitting in a place where she/he can be easily seen by the audience) juggling a clipboard, several lists and a pen. He/she frantically crosses off each item as it is mentioned and between comments tries to scribble additional notes. Person A is chairing the meeting.

A: Good evening, everybody. Do you all have the information pack regarding our new development project? ... Good. I believe this is exactly what our church and community needs. I've already checked the appropriate building regulations, and found out what planning permission and faculties we will require. So I don't see any reason why our committee can't continue to move forward with our plans and then present them to the Church Council for their approval.

B: I can recommend an excellent firm of architects.

A: Actually, I think the church may already have one. However, I'll arrange further meetings with diocesan advisers, heating engineers and lighting consultants to check that they provisionally approve of our ideas, before we formally get plans drawn up and apply for planning permission.

C: We need to research the latest state-of-the-art technology. I feel it's important to install the very best we can afford. I've brought a selection of catalogues for us to look at what lighting and PA systems are available.

A: *(turns to secretary)* Would you mind looking after those for us please? We don't want to mislay them. *(C hands them to the already overloaded secretary.)*

D: And of course we need to check everything we're planning to install is energy-efficient and eco-friendly. We must be environmentally aware, you know.

A: Definitely. What about grant applications? Can anyone come up with a list of charities who may help us with funding? Are you volunteering for that job, Bert? Thank you so much. *(Turns to secretary)* Make a note of that would you?

E: *(hesitantly)* Perhaps we could talk to a reporter from the local paper or radio station. Get ourselves some publicity.

D: We could always put something on the church website or church Facebook page ...

B: Or local businesses may be willing to give us a donation.

C: We need to ask for tenders for all the different types of work required. How many of each do you think we'll need?

B: At least three. Does anybody have any suggestions about reliable local firms to approach? If so, perhaps you could let me know as soon as possible.

A: Well, I think that's probably as much as we can do for now. We'll meet again in a month's time so we can make more definite recommendations to the Church Council and update them on our progress … Does anyone have anything else they'd like to add?

Voice offstage: Yes, I would.

Unless the Lord build the house, they labour in vain that build it.
Unless the Lord remains at the centre of the planning
and discussions,
it is all a waste of time.

A: *(clears throat and looks slightly embarrassed)* Errr, maybe we should close the meeting with a time of prayer …

Kathy Crawford

Note: The author would like to confirm that all the committee members in this sketch are entirely fictional!

You know me, God (Psalm 139)

All: **You know me, God.**
You know me.

A: You see me working.
You see me resting.

B: You know what I think about.
You know what I do.

A: You are everywhere.
Near and far, and all around me.

B: You are in the light
and in the darkness too.

A: You knew me before I was born.
You know how long I will live.

B: Your knowledge is amazing, God.
No one is as wise as you.

A: Take a long look at me, God.
See the good and the bad in me.

B: Let your love grow in me.
Guide me along the road you have made.

Ruth Burgess

I stand in awe (Psalm 139:13–16)

Unbounded God of creation,
You watched me being formed in my mother's womb.
How incredible! How deeply touching that, surrounded
by such marvels of Your making, You yet had eyes
for me, from even before my conception.

I stand in awe of the magnitude of Your being
and Your creation;
I stand in awe of the minuscule detail
of Your concern.

Surely You are God of the intricacies of my body
and of the wholeness of my being.

What more do I require?

Joy Tobler

I will sing (Psalm 146)

As long as I live I will sing.
I will sing to God with my heart and my life and my being and my soul.

I will sing to the God of justice:
a God who addresses inequality,
a God who feeds the hungry,
a God who gets involved.

I will sing to the God of creation:
a God who with risk and courage and wisdom and laughter
made the heavens
and the seas
the octopuses
the dazzling dragonflies
and the fertile earth.

I will sing to the God who is nearer to us than breathing,
the God who notices when a sparrow falls.

I will sing to the God who keeps promises,
who will always judge in favour of the poor,
who will free prisoners,
who will watch over strangers,
who will love and lift up those who have fallen down.

I will sing to the God full of hope.
This is a God I trust.

As long as I live I will sing.
I will sing to God with my heart and my life and my being and my soul.

Ruth Burgess, Spill the Beans

It is good to sing (Psalm 147)

A: It is good to sing to God.

B: It is fun to sing and make music.

A: God gives each star a name.

B: God is in the wind and frost.

A: God makes the grass grow on the hills.

B: God gives the animals their food.

A: God comforts those who are sad.

B: God cares for those who need a home.

A: God enjoys the love of friends.

B: God gives us our daily bread.

Ruth Burgess

Proverbs

Wisdom is shouting out (Proverbs 8:1–12, 18–21)

A version for two voices

Listen, Wisdom is shouting out;
she is making herself heard.

She stands on the hilltops.
She stands at the crossroads.
She stands at the city gates.

Don't miss her.
What she says is important.
Listen up.

I am speaking to you, humanity.
I am speaking to everyone on earth.
Are you immature? Come and learn to be mature.
Are you foolish? Come and learn some sense.
What I will teach you is right and true.
I hate lies.
I will not mislead you.
I will make things clear.
My instructions, my teachings are more valuable than silver and gold.
My experience is better than all the jewels in the world.
I have knowledge and insight.
My judgement is sound.

Listen, Wisdom is shouting out;
she is making herself heard.

She stands high on the hilltops.
She stands at the crossroads.
She stands in your path.

Don't miss her.
She will blow your mind.
Listen now.

I have integrity and honour to gift you.
What you get from me will be better than the finest gold,
more glorious than the purest silver.
I know where to walk.
I follow the paths of justice.
I do what is right.
Those who love me,
those who learn from me,
will fill their lives and houses with treasure.

Listen,
Wisdom is shouting;
She is making herself heard.
Wisdom is calling you out.

Ruth Burgess

You were there (Proverbs 8:22–30)

You were there at the beginning
when God was thinking,
planning, making.

You were a child
handing God a paintbrush,
an architect sharing designs.

The two of you
grew up together:
singing, laughing, playing.

You made a world
full of delight.

Ruth Burgess

What I need (Proverbs 30:7–9)

Don't give me poverty.
Don't give me riches.
Give me what I need.

If I'm poor
I may need to steal to survive.

If I'm rich
I might decide that
I don't need your help.

You know what I need, God.
Keep me honest and truthful.
Give me the life that is right for me.

You know what I need.

Ruth Burgess

An interesting woman (Proverbs 31:10–31)

She's an interesting woman this one:
she does all the household stuff,
sewing, weaving, shopping, cooking ...
supports her partner, feeds their children,
makes sure they have warm clothes ready for the winter.

But there's more to her than that:
she's a landowner, an employer,
a worker, a trader, a benefactress.
She knows the value of her merchandise,
people respect her,
and she's not afraid of the future.

So show her some respect;
she's worthy of it,
she's earned it,
she's a wise woman and a kind one.

Ruth Burgess

Ecclesiastes

I watched and I saw (Ecclesiastes 1–9)

I watched
and I saw
and I understood that there is a time for everything.

There is a time to listen
and a time to speak.

I spoke of justice
and of hopelessness,
of the wisdom of youth
and the foolishness of kings.

I told them to make the most of life,
to share bread with laughter
and to drink wine
with joy.

The preacher, they called me,
the philosopher.

I watched
and I saw
and I understood that there is a time for everybody
and a time for everything.

There is a time to listen
and a time to speak.

And I spoke to them
and I called upon them
to have respect and reverence
for God.

Ruth Burgess

For every moment (Ecclesiastes 3:1)

For everything there is a season,
and a time for every matter under heaven. (Ecc 3:1, NRSV)

For every moment
we will spend dieting,
may we offer twice as many
to feeding the hungry;

for every mile
we put on the treadmill,
may we walk more
in the name of justice;

for every effort we expend
on improving ourselves,
may we seek more opportunities
to change the lives
of those around us.

Thom M Shuman

The words of the philosopher (Ecclesiastes 12:9–13)

Proverbs are as strong
as firmly hammered nails.

Sayings guide us,
like a shepherd guides sheep.

Proverbs can be uncomfortable
and honest.

There is no end
to the writing of books.

Be warned.
Too much study
will wear you out.

So listen.
This is the end of the matter:

We are made
to give God glory.

God knows who we are
and what we are like.

These are the words of the philosopher,
the preacher,
the son of David.

Ruth Burgess

Song of Solomon

My shadow (Song of Solomon 2:2–4)

'I sat down under his shadow with great delight, and his fruit was sweet to my taste. He brought me to the banqueting house, and his banner over me was love' (Song 2:2–4).

I heard a story once of how a man
took umbrage at his shadow – that version
of him that was both him and a perversion.
Thinking to shake his shadow off, he ran

and ran, but still his blacker self clung on.
At length he dropped exhausted to the ground
beneath a spreading tree and – wonder! – found
the tree's great shadow had absorbed his own.

I have a shadow too: a self diminished
by hopes and aspirations unfulfilled,
struggles in and around me, never stilled,
a restless quest for wholeness, never finished.

So: is God's love the overarching tree
whose shade gives rest from self – and joy being me?

Jim Munro

Love sings forever (Song of Solomon 8:6–7)

Many waters cannot quench love,
floods cannot drown it.
Many flames cannot burn love,
raging fires cannot destroy it.
No one can buy love. No one can own it.
Love is as powerful as life and death.
Love sings forever.

Ruth Burgess

Isaiah

Learn to do good (Isaiah 1:17)

Learn to do good; seek justice, rescue the oppressed,
defend the orphan, plead for the widow. (Is 1:17, NRSV)

When we become
lifelong learners
in the ancient
art
of goodness;

when we spend
as much time
searching out the
causes
of injustice,
as we do
online bargains;

when we rally
as quickly around
the homeless
teenager
as we do our
favourite team;

when we attend
the council meetings,
speaking out as
forcefully
for the shelters
to open earlier
this winter
as we did
demanding our
taxes to be cut,

then
we
will find our
way
back to
you.

Thom M Shuman

Here am I (Isaiah 6:1–8)

'Whom shall I send?'
'Here am I; send me!'

Here am I, forgiven,
liberated from my past,
eager and keen to get started.

Here am I, longing to fulfil
the magnitude of
your divine calling.

Here am I,
listening to your voice,
imagination rushing ahead
like a waterfall …
to do what exactly?

Campaign for justice,
bring hope to families,
run a youth club,
welcome strangers, love neighbours,
comfort your homeless and lost,
fundraise to enable your work,
fill congregations, build community …?

Responding, always, to your call.

Did I listen to your detail,
or stop to ask 'How long?'
I am here with you now, Lord,
sad, burnt-out;
not quite what you meant.

Humbly I lay my life at your feet.
I hold my cup for you to fill
only with challenges that
you and I together can manage.

Here I am, Lord,
still and at peace,
comforted by your loving smile
as I resist the rush to cry 'Send me!'

Tricia Creamer

Aunty Jean's change maker (Isaiah 11:1–10)

Andy is sitting reading the Bible, looking worried and pensive as Ada enters.

Andy: Hey, Ada, have you read this stuff?

Ada: Now, Andy, you know I like to do my devotions every morning, of course I've read 'this stuff'!

Andy: It's this guy Isaiah. He must have been on some halle ... halleluciny ... hallelu ... drugs when he wrote some of this.

Ada: I am sure Isaiah would never have taken any kind of hallucinogenics, although he might have had a glass of wine on the odd occasion.

Andy: Come on, Ada, have you read this passage for today about wolves and lambs playing hide and seek with one another?! Hungry cats turning down a free meal of a baby goat! And putting a child in charge of wild and ferocious beasts! Then he comes away with the idea that it would be fine to leave your tiny baby playing in a pit of poisonous snakes! He just has to be on something!

Ada: Oh, I have read it all right.

Andy: So what does it mean? I cannot believe that something like this could ever happen.

Ada: Let me try and explain what I think it means. Remember your Aunty Jean?

Andy: Don't remind me. I remember her being horrible to me. Don't touch this, don't do that, don't do this ... she was called 'Aunty Don't' in the family!

Ada: Aye, she could be pretty ferocious with her possessions, and she used to be quite mean, nasty and horrible to people. She was like that because she herself had had a pretty horrible life and no one ever showed her much kindness as a child, and she was often beaten by her parents when she was younger. She never trusted anyone, until wee Mrs McGlumfer moved into the house next door, and became her friend.

Andy: Aye, Mrs McGlumfer was a lovely wee woman, always kind and generous to all the weans at church.

Ada: Well, Mrs McGlumfer was kind to your Aunty Jean. She was not afraid of her like everybody else, and she did some lovely things for Jean, like bake her wee cakes, and fetch bits of shopping for her, and arranged for her husband to cut Jean's grass when he was cutting theirs. Do you remember how Aunty Jean began to change, because she was being treated with kindness and love? Her heart began to melt a bit, because somebody looked at her differently and did not listen to all the stories that went about the street about yer Aunty Jean.

Andy: Aye, some folk called her a witch and would cross over to the other side of the road when they saw her coming.

Ada: They did, but Mrs McGlumfer never did stuff like that. She tried to look at everybody through God's eyes and found good in them somewhere, and she nurtured the goodness in them, till it began to take root in the person. She got yer Aunty Jean involved in baking, and Aunty Jean started to give you cakes.

Andy: Aye, her apple pies were amazing!

Ada: Not only did she start to bake, but she became a different kind of person towards the end. She herself became more compassionate, more caring and more understanding.

Andy: Aye, so she did.

Ada: Now, Andy, what Isaiah is maybe saying to us this morning is that we need to learn to look at life differently. Find the goodness in people and nurture it, encourage it, water it, until it begins to grow and transform itself from being like a weed to a beautiful flower. All of us have the potential to be something special because that is what God wants for us. All of us can change.

John Murning, Spill the Beans

News summary and weather forecast (Isaiah 35:1–10)

For three readers

A: And now, finally, a summary of the news from Babylon, followed by the weather forecast and traffic and travel.

A new fitness programme designed to strengthen weak hands and feeble knees has been developed by a Hebrew doctor living in Babylon. Volunteers are needed to participate.

The new highway to Jerusalem is due to open tomorrow, having been completed on time and within budget. It will be opened by the first minister and the prophet Isaiah, and is to be called the Holy Way.

Botanists have been excited by the appearance of a new species of crocus in the wilderness. No one is sure where it has come from though its appearance may be linked to the sand and earth displaced whilst the new highway was being built.

Animal behaviour experts have noted the disappearance of lions and jackals in the vicinity of the new highway. There are concerns that their disappearance may eventually lead to repercussions lower down the food chain.

Hoardings near to the new highway have been covered with graffiti. In six-foot-high letters someone has sprayed, somewhat mysteriously, 'Glory, glory, we're going home!' Officials think this may be some kind of code.

And now, over to Gemeti for the weather forecast.

B: Clouds above the desert regions are threatening heavy rain over the next few days and possibly weeks. Continuous rain may result in the appearance of streams in the desert and deep pools of water in wilderness areas. An amber flood warning is in place. Please stay tuned to your local prophets and advisors for more detailed information as to how this may affect you. Our priests suggest that daily prayers to Shamash, the sun god, would not go amiss.

A: And finally over to Ettu for the traffic and travel news.

C: Heavy rainfall may make local roads impassable over the next few days. The new highway, with its built-in flood defence system, is likely to be very busy. Also, reports have been coming in of unpredictable behaviour amongst Hebrew travellers queuing to use the new highway. One correspondent reported 'much singing and leaping and dancing'. Babylonians are being advised not to travel until this outbreak of hysteria calms down. For now, the advice is: if you do not need to travel to Jerusalem – stay at home.

A: This is Babylonian news closing for the night – sleep safely everyone, tomorrow's another day.

Ruth Burgess, Spill the Beans

God promises joy (Isaiah 35)

Despite our fears and anxieties
God promises joy.
Despite our loss and grief
God promises joy.
Despite our neediness and lack of resources
God promises joy.
Despite ourselves
God promises joy.

In the arid places
water will gurgle up,
in the barren places
life will sprout,
frozen wastes
of hearts and lives
will be lovingly thawed
and nurtured
and infused with joy.
We cannot stop it.

God infiltrates our best efforts
and our worst
and causes joy to bubble up
in the hopeless places.

However unlikely it may seem,
be prepared
to experience joy.

Liz Crumlish

Even to your old age (Isaiah 46:4)

Even to your old age I am he, even when you turn grey I will carry you.
I have made, and I will bear; I will carry and will save. (Is 46:4, NRSV)

When others laugh
behind their hands,
you still reach out
to pat the head full
of stress highlights;

when I do the
old-man's-shuffle,
you teach me new
dance steps;

when I lie awake
with memories
tiptoeing through my head,
you read me a sleepy story;

when I close
my eyes for the
last time, I will awake
in your embrace.

Thom M Shuman

When I really thirsted (Isaiah 55:1–5)

When I really thirsted
I came to the waters
and thought they were not there.

Angrily,
if that's still prayer,
I called his name.

He came,
and took me deeper
into the bubbling springs.

Again thirsty
I want to do what satisfies
him and me,
live.

I listen,
and I come
and drink.

Robert Shooter

Soon? (Isaiah 56:1)

Thus says the Lord: Maintain justice, and do what is right,
for soon my salvation will come, and my deliverance be revealed. (Is 56:1)

Soon?
Soon salvation will come?
How about now?
When the darkness seems
as dark as it can be …
now would be good.
Now would be good
for light to come
and dispel the darkness.
Soon.
Please, soon.

Liz Crumlish

The potter and the clay (Isaiah 64:8)

Early in my teaching career (many years ago), I was an art teacher with a specialism in pottery. I loved to create objects in clay and nothing satisfied me more than when I had made something in clay I had dug myself. But it wasn't easy.

First, obviously, messily, the clay had to be dug up. A bucket or two would be more than enough but as you dig don't for a minute imagine the clay emerges ready to use. Not at all! It is always full of impurities: grit, soil, stones, twigs and even the odd wriggly worm. If you leave even a smidgen of these in the clay, after weeks of working, waiting and creating, you will find your lovely pot in fragments at the bottom of the kiln.

How to get rid of the impurities? You put the clay in a bucket, mix water in with it, swill the mixture round and round, until the solid clay becomes a thin liquid, not unlike school custard. You wait, days sometimes, to let all the impurities, heavy bits, sink to the bottom of your bucket, and then you carefully pour off the liquid clay into a fresh bucket.

Is it ready to use? No. It's too wet and has no body, no firmness. You bring it out of its bucket and put it on a 'batt', a rectangle made of plaster of Paris, which draws the water out of the clay. Soon, the drying clay has a 'plastic' texture that you can mould in your fingers.

The next thing you do is to 'wedge' the clay. When you wedge clay, you squeeze it and squash it, folding and refolding it until you have forced out all the little bubbles of air that might be trapped in the body of the clay. You have to do this because if you leave air trapped in your 'objet d'art', the air bubbles will expand in the heat of the kiln and force their way out of the pot. Then the pot breaks into fragments – your dream destroyed.

At last, the clay is ready to use! Get on with it.

Even after you have made your 'objet d'art', you must continue to be patient, tending it until it has fully dried: a slow process. One drop of moisture remaining and guess what will happen? It turns to steam in the kiln and makes its break for freedom. End of pot!

At last, it is ready for firing and, there in the heat of the kiln, the clay is changed forever. Once exposed to the heat, clay undergoes an irreversible chemical change and becomes hard and solid, unchanging.

In other words, you get one shot at making your masterpiece and if it's not right, if it doesn't work out, you can't redeem even the smallest single mistake. No second chances!

When God decides to make a masterpiece, he has all these processes to follow.

First, he must find the clay. Not hard. Not hard, because he has known exactly where he would find this particular lump of clay since day one of creation. I'm the clay, embedded deep in the earth.

Just as my clay was full of impurities, so am I. God slowly and patiently removes all the impurities from me, just as I sought out the sticks and the stones, the soil and the wiggly worms. It may take years to cleanse me, but he is infinitely patient and continues, even if a stray bit of grit suddenly emerges to make him start over again. He won't get tired and give up on me, and will prepare me, the clay, until he judges it ready to shape his masterpiece.

Imagine being held in God's hands, being measured and moulded, examined and scrutinised until the task is finished.

Just imagine! God will sigh over the perfection in me!

Colin Taylor

No matter how stubborn (Isaiah 65:1)

I was ready to be sought out by those who did not ask, to be found
by those who did not seek me. I said, 'Here I am, here I am'
to a nation that did not call on my name. (Is 65:1, NRSV)

No matter how
stubborn
we are, you
are flexible;

however often we
refuse to say
your name, you
whisper ours;

wherever we long
to flee from you,
you are waiting
for us, just
around the corner
with your hope.

Thom M Shuman

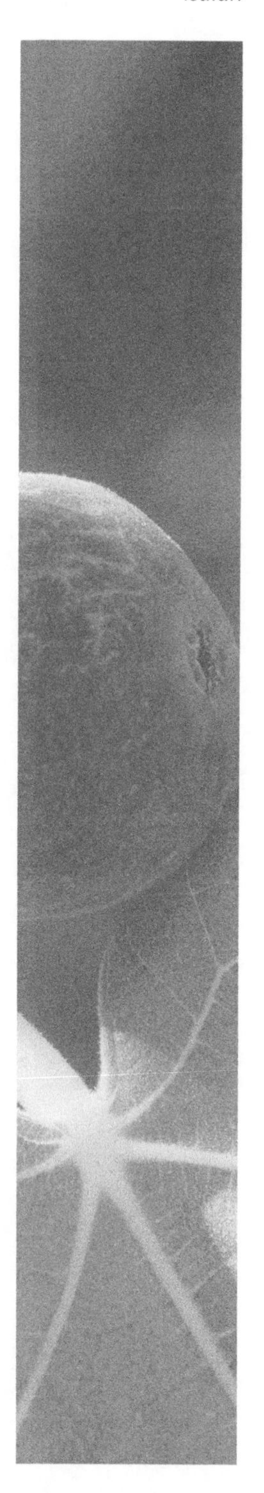

Be glad (Isaiah 65:18)

But be glad and rejoice forever in what I am creating;
for I am about to create Jerusalem as a joy,
and its people as a delight. (Is 65:18, NRSV)

Where we see
rotting neighbourhoods,
you envision
communities of hope;

where we hear
the echoes of
empty concrete canyons,
you listen to the
laughter of children
in the playgrounds;

as we wander down
streets littered
with despair, we
find you picking
up lives and creating
joy in broken hearts.

Thom M Shuman

This is the one (Isaiah 66:2b)

But this is the one to whom I will look, to the humble and contrite in spirit, who trembles at my word. (Is 66:2b, NRSV)

Terror
fear
debt
doubt
death can all
knock us down,
but
if we reach
out our shaky hands
to grasp your
Word,

you will draw us
into
your embrace of
hope and life.

Thom M Shuman

Jeremiah

I am only (Jeremiah 1:4–10)

I am only, I do not know
how or what or where;

I am only, I cannot go:
I am too afraid.

I am only, I have not
height or voice or strength;

I am only, I am little,
broken, old, young.

I am only, I will not
be welcomed, heard or heeded;

I am only, they are more,
so much more than me.

I am only, but I am listening.
I will trust you when you call;

for I am only who I am,
and with you I am not alone.

Sarah Agnew

I remember (Jeremiah 2:2)

I remember the devotion of your youth, your love as a bride, how you followed me in the wilderness, in a land not sown. (Jer 2:2, NRSV)

I remember when
I was a little
child,
clinging so tightly
to you,

determined never,
ever to let go, for
fear of losing you;

I remember those
promises
I made, holding hands
with you, looking
you in the eyes
with a passion
which seemed to
dim the full moon
shining through
the window;

I remember following
you with unfettered
enthusiasm,
carefully placing my
feet in the impressions
you left
in my heart,
convinced you knew
a path I could not see;

I remember
and wonder
why
did I

forget?

Thom M Shuman

On the shop floor (Jeremiah 7:2)

Stand in the gate of the Lord's house, and proclaim there this word, and say, 'Hear the word of the Lord, all you people of Judah, you that enter these gates to worship the Lord.' (Jer 7:2, NRSV)

Let us stand
on the shop floor
and declare,
'Let this be the
place where
each person
is paid fairly';

let us stand
in the emergency room
and say aloud,
'Let this be the
place where
people get the
medical care
they not only need,
but deserve';

let us stand
in the classrooms
and make known,
'Let this be the
place where
children will
receive a first-class
education,
no matter their
status in society';

let us stand
in every place,
next to every person;
with you, Lord,
let us stand.

Thom M Shuman

May this day (Jeremiah 17:24)

But if you listen to me, says the Lord, and bring in no burden by the gates of this city on the Sabbath day, but keep the Sabbath day holy and do no work on it. (Jer 17:24, NRSV)

May this day
have less running
around
with errands, and
more
walking with you;

may this day
offer less talking
and
more silence;

may this day
be less about
accumulating
and more about
giving (away);

may this day
contain less
grumbling
and more
songs
to you;

may this day
be less focused
on me, and
more on the ones I
love (especially
you);

may this day
be less about
doing and
more about
being;
may this day
be Sabbath.

Thom M Shuman

Burning truth (Jeremiah 36)

Jeremiah: Right, Baruch, let's go over what's happened. First, you went to the temple?

Baruch: Yes. I took the scroll and waited while the people gathered. Then I read it to them.

Jeremiah: All of it?

Baruch: All of it, yes. It took … quite some time.

Jeremiah: And they listened? How did they seem to react?

Baruch: If anything, the crowd grew closer – and bigger – the more I read. It was a fast day, and it was rumoured that even those who had never fasted with much sincerity before had been solemnly fasting.

Jeremiah: A good sign then. A sign of change.

Baruch: Yes. A real desire for the Lord. A recognition of the need to return to God's ways.

Jeremiah: Then the officials heard about it?

Baruch: That's right. They could not have been unaware of the talk, the very public shows of penance. Some people were weeping in the temple all night! One of the officials reported to a meeting of the court staff at the palace.

Jeremiah: And they called you in?

Baruch: Yes. I was asked to read it all a second time, to the officials.

Jeremiah: But they reacted somewhat differently from the townspeople?

Baruch: Yes. They were alarmed; unnerved. When I'd finished reading, they just stared at me, and at each other, for a long time. It was a very uncomfortable silence.

Jeremiah: Were you afraid, my son?

Baruch: It was what I expected. These are harder words for our leaders to hear than the people. It is harder to expect them to listen and to change. Even when it is the Lord speaking, not you or I.

Jeremiah: What did they say? What broke their silence?

Baruch: Several of them began to mutter all at once, saying, 'We must tell the king. We must tell the king!'

Jeremiah: But they didn't want you to be the one to read to the king?

Baruch: No. They took the scroll away from me.

Jeremiah: And let you go?

Baruch: They gave me a piece of advice first.

Jeremiah: Oh?

Baruch: That's when they said we should go into hiding.

Jeremiah: Ah yes. Well, no harm in heeding that, is there?

Baruch: I've had word that they are looking to arrest us.

Jeremiah: Yes, yes. But tell me again about what happened when they read to the king. What is it you heard?

Baruch: It was Jehudi who read the scroll to the king. He was in the winter palace. You know how cold these nights are, this time of year …

Jeremiah: Yes. So the fire was lit.

Baruch: That's right. The fire was lit. And every time the scroll was hanging down beyond Jehudi's elbow, the king lunged for it with a knife, ripping the end off and throwing it in the fire.

Jeremiah: But what did all the others do? Did they just stand by?

Baruch: No! They tried to stop him. They begged the king to stop!

Jeremiah: How brave. They must have known they were risking their lives … That is a hopeful sign, a very hopeful sign.

Baruch: Yes, but they couldn't stop him. Not the king. He paid no attention to their protests. He burned the whole scroll. All of it! All of the Lord's words to us!

Jeremiah: That means just one thing then.

Baruch: It means the Lord's message is gone.

Jeremiah: No. God will find deeper ways to get through to us, I'm sure. We don't need written words to know what's right and wrong. The king can burn scrolls and arrest prophets, but he can't take away the call for change.

Baruch: But how will the people hear that call now?

Jeremiah: Until the Lord shows another way, we'd better get back to writing.

Baruch: What? Do it all again?

Jeremiah: You read it completely twice through, my son, and I know the strength of your memory.

Baruch: All right. Take two, here we come. You're right. I know much of it by heart …

Jo Love, Spill the Beans

Lamentations

God's love is steadfast (Lamentations 3:22–26)

God's love is strong and steadfast.
God's mercy never comes to an end.

Sure as the sun's rising is God's mercy.
New every morning is God's love.

God is everything we have.
We put our hope in God.

God sees when we are treated unfairly.
God knows when our courts are corrupt.

God hears us cry when we are in trouble.
God tells us not to be afraid.

God is everything we have.
We put our hope in God.

When we feel trapped and forgotten,
when we feel that hope is gone,

we need to tell ourselves again and again,
God's love and mercy never ends.

God is everything we have.
We put our hope in God.

Ruth Burgess

The shame of God's people (Lamentations 5)

Remember, O God, what has happened to us.
Look at us and see our disgrace.

Our fathers have been taken and killed.
All our mothers are widows.

Our wives have been raped on the mountains.
Our daughters have been forced to submit.

Our old people are shown no respect.
Our children no longer make music.

Happiness has gone from our lives.
We can hardly see through our tears.

Bring us back to you, God, bring us back,
or have you forgotten us forever?

Ruth Burgess

Ezekiel

Ezekiel's vision (Ezekiel 1–2)

The strong hand of God fell upon me,
and out of the north, a wind blew:
a dark cloud with brilliant light round it,
and out of it, sharp lightning flew.
The heart of the darkness was glowing,
like bronze when it flows in white flame;
and deep in the glow were four creatures,
moving fast though the storm as it came.

Like humans the creatures stood upright,
but each had four wings spreading wide;
and hooves like an ox, brightly gleaming;
and two human hands at their sides.
The face of a human looked forward,
the face of a lion looked right;
the face of a bull looked to leftward,
the face of an eagle behind.

I watched them like thunderbolts racing,
their paths never turning aside.
Four wheels made of gemstone moved with them,
the rim of each one filled with eyes.
Above was a high vault like sapphire,
beneath it their wings rose and fell;
and then with a sound like a battle
they folded their wings, and were still.

A throne was set high on the sapphire
and on it a form like a man;
he glittered like bronze high above me,
above and below him, light shone.
The light shone around him like rainbows,
and there I heard voice upon voice
sing: 'Yahweh is blessed in creation
and earth is his own dwelling place.'

Roddy Cowie

V is for ... (Ezekiel 37:1–14)

Eccchhhh.

Eccchhhh.

Morning, Vinnie.

Morning, Vic.

Nice and sunny.

Always nice and sunny in the wilderness, Vic.

What you doing today, Vinnie?

Thought I'd fly over the valley of dry bones, Vic. I hear there's been something going on over there.

Nah, nothing happens there, the bones are long dead, not a morsel of meat on them. Nothing for us, Vinnie, nothing at all.

Ah, but I've heard a rumour.

A rumour, what's that?

A story – I've heard a story about that valley – and it sounds interesting.

Who did you hear the story from?

From Vikki – she often flies over there – it's on her patch.

Go on.

Well, she said that one day when she was flying over she saw a man there.

Just one man: he wouldn't last long in the wilderness – could be good news for us ...

But there's more, Vic.

Go on.

This man seemed to be talking to someone, like he was having a conversation, but there was no one else there.

Ah, the wilderness does strange things to humans. He was probably imagining stuff, seeing stuff that wasn't there, Vinnie.

And then the man shouted across the valley.

Did he shout anything interesting?

He shouted to the bones – God says this – 'I'm going to bring you back to life – cover you with muscles and sinews and skin and then you'll know that I'm God.'

Interesting – quite mad – but interesting.

But Vikki said it happened – there was a rattling noise and the bones began to join together – and they put on muscles and flesh and were covered in skin.

Are you sure Vikki is OK? She's not had indigestion and a strange dream or something?

She sounded fine – and she said that then the man shouted again.

And?

And he told the wind that God had commanded it to come to the wilderness and breathe life into the bodies.

And don't tell me the wind came!

It came from every direction and blew into the bodies and they came to life – there were enough of them to make an army!

And then what happened?

The man shouted that he was going back to his people and that he was going to tell them that they were like old dry bones.

They'd love that!

But then he'd tell them that God would blow his breath into them, and give them all new life.

So did this man find his way out of the wilderness and go back to his home and leave all these people in the valley?

Vikki doesn't know. She was a bit spooked by the wind and the rattling bones and she flew away.

So?

So I thought that it might be worth flying over to the valley and seeing if this army of people is still there.

Did Vikki mention food or water in her dream?

She said it wasn't a dream, but no she didn't.

So some of these people might have got lost and might have died in the wilderness and there might still be flesh on their bones.

There might.

Definitely worth having a look at this rumour of yours, Vinnie. If there's anything in it, we could be feasting for days. Let's be flying ...

Sure thing, Vic.

Eccchhhh.

Eccchhhh.

Ruth Burgess

Note: Reference for research into vulture sounds!: https://www.youtube.com/watch?v=uA5yGyB_z5U

Daniel

Ashpenaz gets the jitters (Daniel 1)

Fingers crossed.
Touch wood.
Quick prayer.
Clutch lucky amulet.

Those Jewish lads look pretty healthy to me
even though they refused the gourmet banquets
and opted for peasant-style turnip stews.

Let's hope his nibs doesn't throw a wobbly.
Um ... I mean
I'm sure his divine majesty will approve of the initiative I have taken.

If it goes wrong, what shall I do?
Throw myself on his mercy?
That's so small I'd be certain to miss.
Quick camel ride to the border?
His majesty has, I know, many fascinating ways
of terminating a subject's existence.
And I'd rather not experience any of them first hand.

Phew!
It worked.
He was actually pleased.
Rewarded me.
Which god shall I thank?
Yahweh, the Jewish lads' deity?
Or one of ours?
Or both,
just to be on the safe side?

Brian Ford

Come out of there (Daniel 3)

A long time ago, in a country called Babylon, there was a king who had a very long name. He was called King Nebuchadnezzar. King Nebuchadnezzar was a powerful king, and when he wanted something to happen – it did!

One day King Nebuchadnezzar decided that he wanted a golden statue built. When it was finished it was enormous. It was twenty-seven metres high – as high as two double-decker buses standing on top of each other – and nearly three metres wide – as wide as a train carriage. It was huge.

King Nebuchadnezzar decided that the statue was so huge and so important that all his people should get down on their knees and pray to it. And he decided that he would have a special day to tell the people about the statue.

To make the day special King Nebuchadnezzar called together his royal orchestra and told them that they were to play as loudly as they could. There were trumpeters and harp players and oboe players and zither players and probably a lot of drummers as well. They could make lots of noise.

The special day arrived. All the important people of Babylon stood in front of the huge golden statue. They were impressed. Then the king's herald announced, 'As soon as you hear the music playing you are to get down on your knees and pray to the statue. And anyone who does not do this will be tied up and thrown into the fiery furnace!'

The fiery furnace was very hot. It had been used to melt the gold to make the statue. Anybody who was thrown into it would die very very quickly.

So the king gave a signal, and the music played – it was deafening – and all the people got on their knees and prayed to the statue. Well, not quite all the people because there were three men who did not get down on their knees; they just stood there. And, of course, somebody went and told the king.

King Nebuchadnezzar was angry. He thought that everyone should do what he told them to do. How dare these men disobey his command! He sent for the three men and they were brought before him.

When he saw them the king recognised who the men were. They were from another country but had been brought up in Babylon. They were Jews with responsible jobs in Babylon and they worshipped a different god to King Nebuchadnezzar. They were called Shadrach, Meshach and Abednego.

The king glared at them and said: 'If you do not bow down and worship my statue when the music plays I will have you thrown into the fiery furnace. Do you think any god can save you?'

And Shadrach, Meshach and Abednego answered him: 'If the God we serve is able to save us from the fiery furnace he will. But even if he doesn't, we will not worship your gold statue.'

The king was mad. Nobody was allowed to say no to him. He really lost his temper. He stamped his feet. His face turned red. And he ordered the strongest men in his army to tie up Shadrach, Meshach and Abednego and to throw them into the blazing furnace. And because he was so cross he ordered that the furnace be heated seven times hotter than it was usually heated.

So they tied Shadrach, Meshach and Abednego up, fully dressed, and threw them into the middle of the furnace. And the flames were so hot that they burned the men who threw them in.

The king looked on. All the other people who had knelt and prayed to the golden statue watched as well.

And then the king saw that something had happened. He went a little closer to the furnace and looked in.

'What's going on? I can see four, not three, men in the furnace,' he said. 'And they're not tied up. They're walking around unharmed. And the fourth man – he looks like an angel.'

And King Nebuchadnezzar stood outside the door of the furnace and shouted: 'Shadrach! Meshach! Abednego! Servants of the greatest God! Come out of there!'

And Shadrach, Meshach and Abednego walked out of the furnace unharmed. The king and the court officials gathered round to examine the men. They were not hurt. Their hair was not singed. Their clothes were not burnt. There was not even the smell of smoke on them. And the fourth man had disappeared.

King Nebuchadnezzar was amazed, and he said: 'Praise be to the God of Shadrach, Meshach and Abednego! He sent his angel to rescue these men who trust him and serve him. They disobeyed my commands and risked their lives rather than bow down and worship any god except their own. No one is to disrespect this God. He is the greatest God. There is no other God who can rescue people like this.'

And King Nebuchadnezzar promoted Shadrach, Meshach and Abednego to even better jobs in the province of Babylon.

Ruth Burgess

Note: There is a great musical version of this story by Louis Armstrong and his band. 'Shadrach, Meshach, Abednego':
https://www.youtube.com/watch?v=6r1baNdglmo

Fiery furnace rap (Daniel 3)

The king sent out a decree one day:
'When you hear the sound of music you must obey;
you must bow down to the image of gold –
or else you'll burn if you don't do what you're told.'

But Shadrach, Meshach and Abednego,
Shadrach, Meshach and Abednego,
Shadrach, Meshach and Abednego
turned to the king and said, 'No! No! No!'

The king was angry and asked them how
they thought they'd escape if they did not bow.
He said, 'I'll throw you into the fire to burn
if to my gods you will not turn.'

But Shadrach, Meshach and Abednego ...

Shadrach, Meshach and Abednego
replied to the king that the answer was no.
'Our God is greater than an image of gold.
He'll save us from the fire ... so that's you told!'

Yes, Shadrach, Meshach and Abednego …

The king was raging and ordered that the fire
be lit up and heated up to seven times higher.
The three were firmly bound and thrown into the flames.
'Aha,' said the king, 'that's an end to their games.'

For Shadrach, Meshach and Abednego …

The king then peeked in the furnace door.
'How come,' he said, 'there are not three but four?
An angel of God has loosed their chains –
I think it's pretty obvious that their God reigns!'

Shadrach, Meshach and Abednego,
they were the men whose answer was no.
They risked their lives in the terrible flame,
but lived to praise God's wonderful name.

Shadrach, Meshach and Abednego,
they were the men who said, 'No! No! No!'

Marjory J.B. Williamson

Hungry? (Daniel 6)

Hungry?
Of course we were hungry.
The palace staff kept us hungry.
Made us more vicious, they said.

And when they threw a man down to us
that particular night
we were ready to tear him limb from limb
and feast.

But before we reached him
another man appeared –
our lucky night, we thought –
but suddenly we were no longer hungry,
just sleepy;
we couldn't keep our eyes open.

Early the next morning
they pulled the first man out of our pit,
unharmed,
we hadn't even scratched him.
And the second man had disappeared.

Hungry?
We were starving.
Even hungrier than the night before!

And then –
glory! –
they threw men
and women
and children
into our pit –
breakfast,
elevenses,
lunch,
tea
and dinner
and midnight snacks
for nights and days to come.

Ruth Burgess

Hosea

I am Gomer (Hosea 1:2–10)

I am Gomer, a woman with a reputation. 'A wife of whoredom' I was called! That's not very nice.

At the time I lived, honour, men's honour, was important. No matter if it wasn't the woman's fault. A woman like me, whose reputation was tarnished, would harm a man's honour, would not be good marriage material.

So I married the prophet Hosea. We were quite an odd couple. People wondered what he saw in me. Did he marry me just as some kind of preaching aid? They also might have wondered what I saw in him – a religious guy who says he's a prophet didn't look much like my type either.

People always say that our marriage, and our children's strange names, are symbolic of God's love of an unfaithful people. But to us it was so much more than that. In life sometimes you have to give someone a chance. In relationships there is something more important than honour and reputation. Did people consider that maybe we actually liked each other?!

Our marriage wasn't always easy. People would point fingers and mutter behind our backs. But Hosea said to take no notice. He said that they had been unfaithful in so many ways to what God wants. He said that, despite the difficult start to our marriage, how we cared for each other and our children would show them how God cared for his people, and teach them something about God's mercy.

Liz Delafield

Sow righteousness (Hosea 10:12–14)

'Sow righteousness.'
And you will never know what might spring up.

Our headlines are a harvest of everything but.
The old book warns us not to trust in horses.
Well, the horses have long gone.
They have given way to bigger threats,

violence wreaking vengeance from the sky.
War is good business.
It's just tough when the innocent get in the way.

But out of sight the sowing of good seed
continues to be the offering of the ordinary
who never make the news.
Small gifts of kindness shown to neighbour
and to stranger bind us together
in a belonging that is shared.
Those with the least are so often the ones
to live the giving of hospitality.
They are the ones who provide windows into neighbourhoods
where righteousness and peace kiss each other.

Our worship and all our holy talk are discordant drivel
unless justice flows like a river and righteousness
runs like a stream that never dries up.

'Sow righteousness.'
And we will never know what might spring from our parched land.

John Randall

What kind of God? (Hosea 11:1–9)

What kind of God?

God the warrior,
God the destroyer,
God the Almighty?

God the befriender,
God the tender one,
God the lover?

God the holy one,
God the angry one,
God the judge?

God, creator of the universe,
God the mysterious,
God who knows us by name?

What kind of God do we worship?
What kind of God do we pray to?
What kind of God loves us?
Which story of God haunts us?
Which chapters of the Bible do we read?

If we are looking for a touchstone,
a yardstick,
a benchmark,
we need to read Hosea.

Hosea tells us that God is
full of integrity
and healing
and loving kindness.

God nurtures us
and understands us.

God is holy.
God says 'I am with you.'

God knows us
and loves us
and will not stop loving us.

That's amazing!
Let creation shout glory!

God knows us
and loves us
and will not stop loving us

for ever and ever
and ever.
Amen

Ruth Burgess, Spill the Beans

Jessie and Ben (Hosea 11:1–9)

Jessie had a little brother – who was sometimes a very naughty little brother, and he was called Ben. Ben was often in trouble. If there were fingerprints in the icing on the cake or biscuit crumbs all over the sofa, or a broken cup in the kitchen – it was likely to be Ben who had done it.

Once Ben had gone into Jessie's bedroom and found her felt pens and scribbled on her favourite poster and then left the tops off the pens so that they had all dried up.

Another day Ben had borrowed Jessie's second favourite T-shirt and got grass stains all over it and left it in a crumpled heap at the bottom of the laundry basket.

There were times when Jessie wished to be an only child!

And yet Jesse could remember back to when Ben was born and how tiny he had seemed when her mum brought him home from the hospital. She could remember him clinging on to her finger, and later holding her hand as he learned to walk. She remembered his first words and how proud she had been when he had learnt to say her name.

And yesterday Ben had cuddled up to her on the sofa whilst they were watching the television and he had fallen fast asleep in her arms and she had carried him up to bed.

Jessie was Ben's big sister and she loved him. There were times when he made her cross but she could not imagine life without him.

Jessie looked forward to being around Ben as he grew up.

Jessie was Ben's big sister. And whether Ben was being good or bad, Jessie loved him.

Ruth Burgess, Spill the Beans

Joel

After the locusts (Joel 1, 2)

Joel the prophet lived a long time ago. He had the very important job of listening to God and telling his friends what God was saying, and of listening to his friends and telling God what his friends were saying.

Many of Joel's friends were farmers. There was Enan who grew corn. There was Abi who had a grapevine. There was Merari who took care of the olive trees. There were Asha and Zeb who planted tomatoes and cucumbers and melons and pomegranates. There was Ira the shepherd and Obed who kept cows. They worked hard growing food in their fields and looking after their animals. Every year they looked forward to harvest time. It was always so wonderful to cut the corn, milk the cows and pick all the grapes – and make wine and bread for a big feast to say thank you to God!

But one year, as harvest time was coming, there was a terrible disaster. A huge swarm of flying, buzzing insects came swooping over all the fields. Locusts! There were thousands of them! No – millions of them! They were everywhere! Joel could hardly go outside without locusts getting in his hair and under his feet, flying and buzzing all round. They were small creatures, but with their tiny sharp teeth they began to eat everything they could find. They munched Enan's corn and nibbled Abi's grapes. They chewed up Merari's olives and even gnawed the bark off the trees. They gobbled up Zeb and Asha's juicy fruits and tasty vegetables. Then they landed on the grass that the sheep and cows liked to eat, and they chomped all the grass too.

'Dear God!' cried Joel, 'we're going to starve! Look – the locusts have polished off all our food! They've scoffed the lot! They've wolfed down everything – there's nothing left for us to eat! Even the cows are mooing in hunger, and the sheep are bleating because their bellies are empty!'

'My dear Joel,' said God, 'tell everyone not to panic. I know this is a hard time for you. I am going to send plenty of rain to get the grass growing again. It won't be long before your fields are full of corn, and you're busy making wine and olive oil. Everything that the locusts took away, I will give back to you in a new harvest. And I'll give you something more special than food – I'll give you my Spirit, so that you can dream of how wonderful the world can be!'

So Joel told his friends what God was saying. And instead of feeling scared and worried, Joel's friends trusted God's promise and looked forward to their new harvest and their wonderful dreams.

Jo Love, Spill the Beans

The aftermath (Joel 2:1–32)

For three voices. Said as if surveying the devastated land after the locust swarm.

A: Is it over?

B: Have they gone?

C: Can I bear to look?

A: Oh ... my ... God.

B: Would you look at this.

C: I can't take in what I'm seeing.

A: The darkness – at least that's gone.

B: And the noise.

C: I've never known anything like it.

A: They sounded like fire crackling.

B: They blotted out the sun.

C: They filled the air like a crazed silver snowstorm.

A: They covered the land, settling and soaring up on field and vineyard and orchard, whirling like dead leaves in an autumn storm.

B: Buzzing wings and cutting teeth by the million, scorching the earth with no mercy.

C: Their power and ferocity overwhelmed us, and we stand mocked by creatures we could crush by the fistful and trample underfoot.

A: There was corn ripe for harvest here, tall and gold.

B: There were grapes weighing down the branches of the vine.

C: Over there, there were figs swelling on the trees and clustered olives turning from green to black.

A: Our livestock were at pasture.

B: We had milk and meat enough to feast.

C: It was going to be a great day in the temple.

A: We were holding up despite the poor rains, but these swarming armies came without warning and tore apart everything we planted and tended.

B: The fields – look at them – nothing but bare earth. Not one stalk of wheat left standing, not one ear of barley to be found in the dust.

C: The vines are stripped naked. The trees stand white and exposed without bark or foliage.

A: We watched them come with the wind and descend like a plague.

B: They rushed against us, robbing and ravaging everything we had.

C: And we could do nothing … nothing … to stop them.

A: There will be no wine and no bread.

B: Do you hear the cattle, bellowing with hunger, like voices for our grief.

C: The priests hold night-long vigils, but can only weep.

A: What can we do?

B: Bow our heads and spread out to God our useless empty hands, with nothing to offer but our broken hearts.

C: What hope will God bring us now?

Jo Love, Spill the Beans

Dreams and visions (Joel 2:28–29)

In the Book of Joel
are these words:

God said I will pour out my spirit
on everyone.

Your sons and your daughters will proclaim my message.
Old people will have dreams.
Young people will see visions.
I will pour out my spirit on everyone.

Dreams can be worked at.
Dreams can become reality.
Remember Martin Luther King?
Remember his dream?

Dreams
Visions
Hopes
Yearnings.

What are your dreams:
for yourself …
for your friends …
for your family?

What are your dreams:
for your church …
for your community …
for your country?

What are your dreams:
for the environment …
for the world's children …
for peace?

Dreams
Plans

Possibilities
Longings.

Take time for thinking
Take time for looking
Take time for listening
Take time to dream.

Ruth Burgess, Spill the Beans

Somewhere to play (Joel 2:28–29)

Martin wanted somewhere to play. He lived in a big city. There were lots of streets full of houses. Not many people had gardens because the houses had been built very close together. There were streets full of shops. There were busy roads and lots of cars. There were car parks. There was a school with a playground, but the gate to the playground was locked when the school wasn't open. There was a park, but it was a long way away and it was more for sitting in than playing in.

Not very far away there was an old house called Applegarth which was falling down. Around the house was a big garden. Martin and his friends sometimes played in the garden, but last week some people had come and put up a big fence around the garden. Martin had asked one of the people what was happening and the person told him that soon the house was going to be pulled down and a new supermarket and car park built on the site.

Martin had gone home and talked to his mum. Why build a supermarket? They already had a big one down the road and there was no need for another one.

His mum had agreed. They talked about all the problems Martin was having finding somewhere to play, and then Martin's mum said, 'Perhaps you could write to the council.'

Martin wasn't quite sure what this meant, but his mum explained to him that the people who made decisions about what could be built in the city were the council. It was their job to listen to what people thought about the things that happened in the city and then to decide what to do.

Martin's mum said that sometimes people sent a petition to the council. This meant that they found lots of people who agreed with what they were saying and got them to sign a piece of paper to say so.

Martin and his mum decided to make a petition. They worked out what to put on the paper. At the top it said:

Children in this city need somewhere safe to play. We don't need another supermarket. Why can't Applegarth be turned into a park?

Martin took the paper round his friends and neighbours and nearly everybody signed it and wrote down their address. Lots of people heard about the petition and Martin printed out more pages, and lots more people signed. In two weeks there were 1374 names on the pages.

Martin's mum rang up one of the councillors, and she said that she would come round to Martin's house and collect the petition. Martin's mum rang the local paper and Martin invited lots of his friends round and a photographer arrived, and in the local paper that week was a picture of Martin and the councillor and Martin's friends waving pages of the petition.

The councillor told Martin that she would take the petition to the next council meeting. Martin is going with his mum to the meeting to see what happens.

Martin's dream about a safe place to play might come true.

Ruth Burgess, Spill the Beans

Amos

Let justice roll (Amos 5)

For two voices

Seek good and not evil.
Hate evil, love good.
Establish justice at your gate.

I do not want songs, says God.
I do not want offerings.
I will not listen to your music.

Seek good and not evil.
Hate evil, love good.
Establish justice at your gate.

Let justice roll!
Let it crash down like a high waterfall.
Let it dance like a mountain stream.

Let right living roll!
Let it be valued in your courts.
Let it be practised in your homes.

Seek good and not evil.
Hate evil, love good.

God will be with you.

God will be with you.

Let justice roll! *(both voices)*

Ruth Burgess

I am not a prophet (Amos 5–9)

I am not a prophet.
I am not a prophet's son.
I look after the fig trees.
I herd the sheep and goats.
God took me from my daily work.

God gave me a new job to do.
God ordered me to speak to the nation.
God has sent me to speak the truth.

God says, 'You have cheated the poor.
You have sold honest people into slavery.
You have taken clothes as a security for debt.
You are not living by my laws.'

'Woe to those who take bribes,' says God,
'who stretch out on couches and feast.
A day of disaster is coming.
Your behaviour is bringing it on.'

God says, 'I will shake this nation.
I will shake them like wheat in a sieve.
I will sift out all who are worthless.
Only those who do good will remain.'

I am not a prophet.
I am not a prophet's son.
I speak the words that God tells me.
Listen to the judgements of God.

Ruth Burgess

Obadiah

A day will come (Obadiah 12–15, 21)

Do not gloat
over the misfortune of others.

Do not stand at the crossroads
and ambush those who are running for their lives.

Do not be happy
when you see people in trouble.

Do not laugh at them
in their suffering and distress.

A day will come
when you will be treated
as you have treated other people.

The earth
and all its people
belong to God.

Ruth Burgess

Jonah

One day (Jonah 1–4)

One day Jonah was sitting down, when God spoke to him and said, 'Jonah, go to the city of Nineveh and tell the people to stop being bad and turn over a new leaf or I will destroy the city and kill everyone.'

Jonah decided to argue so he said, 'God, I will not go today because it's not the weather for travelling, and even if I did go, you would probably not do it and make me look a right fool.'

God was angry, and said, 'Jonah. Go!'

Jonah saw that he had better shut up.

Jonah walked to Joppa in the hot sun and he was getting very cross. He decided he would not go to Nineveh. He would get on a boat and go somewhere else and hide.

Jonah went below to his cabin and was so tired he fell asleep. The ship sailed well for a while and then all of a sudden there began a terrible storm. The captain was getting worried so he ordered everyone to pray to their gods. He went downstairs to wake Jonah up, and when he told Jonah what had happened Jonah told the captain what he'd done. Jonah told the captain to throw him overboard. The captain would not. The captain told Jonah to pray. Jonah did, but nothing happened, so Jonah was thrown overboard.

Jonah was floating on his back when he was swallowed by a whale. He was very cold inside the whale so Jonah prayed to God to let him out. This God did. Jonah was pleased and prayed to God thanking him. Jonah went straight to the city of Nineveh and told everyone the message. At first nobody believed him and they all laughed at him, but there was something about this man that changed their minds. The message got to the king and he told everyone to change their ways. Within forty days, this everyone did. So God forgave them and everyone was happy, except for Jonah.

Jonah was complaining, 'What was the good of me coming? I knew you wouldn't do it. It never happened. Now I'm going to sit here and die.'

God heard this and made a tree grow near Jonah. For a day Jonah sat in the shade of the tree. The next day the tree withered up and died.

Jonah was very unhappy and said, 'Why did that tree wither up and die? I liked it.'

God said to Jonah, 'You felt sorry for the tree like I did for those people.'

Jonah saw God's point and got up and went home happily.

Christopher, aged 10

Sailor's tale (Jonah 1–4)

Ash: Hey, Mushi! Good trip?

Mushi: No. Not a good trip.

Ash: Oh? Rough waters?

Mushi: You could say that.

Ash: The news that came back yesterday was of an unusual calm after quite a storm. You got caught in it too then?

Mushi: Yes … yes, we did.

Ash: Well, it's not the first squally night and it won't be the last, eh! You've survived it again!

Mushi: This time was different, Ash. I don't want to sail those waters again as long as I live.

Ash: What do you mean? When has a storm ever rocked you? You handle the big boats better than anyone – in any weather! Of course you'll be back out there!

Mushi: No, I mean it, Ash. My sailing days are done. In fact, my living days are done. I'm done.

Ash: What's got into you? What happened out there?

Mushi: I've killed a man.

Ash: What?!

Mushi: You heard me. I'm a murderer. My days are up. I'll pay for it, I'm sure.

Ash: What happened, Mushi? An accident surely.

Mushi: I didn't mean it – I didn't want to do it, but he said it was the only way.

Ash: Stop! Stop and tell me what this is all about.

Mushi: Were you here the day we were loading up? Do you remember the wee guy running about the place? Nobody knew him. He heard we were heading west and he was desperate to come with us. So we let him on the boat at the last minute: he had good money for the ride.

Ash: The wee guy with the black goatskin and tassels on his coat? He can't have gone with you!

Mushi: Yep, that was him. And he was with us, yes.

Ash: Mushi, that's impossible! He showed up again yesterday. Well, we found him at dawn, asleep on the beach.

Mushi: That's impossible! Ash, I killed him! I threw him overboard. But he made me do it. The gods were angry with someone. The sea was going crazy. We tried to lighten our load by throwing over half the cargo, but it didn't help. Then he said it was his fault, and we all yelled, 'What have you done, man?!' He just yelled that he was running away and that we had to throw him over or the storm would kill us all. We wouldn't do it. We tried to row back, we tried everything, but in the end it was me who did it. I pushed him over the side, into the sea. He disappeared, Ash, he went right under, gone, just like that. I killed him. I killed that poor man.

Ash: This isn't making any sense ... Do you remember anything else about what he looked like, what he was wearing?

Mushi: Yes. His headband. It was silk. I was staring at it as he was shouting at me.

Ash: Silk? Purple silk? And his hair is still pure black but –

Mushi: But his beard is going grey ...

They stare at each other in disbelief. Pause.

Mushi: No! How could he have survived? How did he get back here?

Ash: How much longer did the storm last?

Mushi: No time at all. He went under and the waters went still.

Ash: Wow! Who is his god?

Mushi: He called his god the Maker of heaven and earth. Maybe he was right. We made our offerings and promised our devotion. Taking no chances, not after that.

Ash: He must have been saved somehow. There was nearly a beached whale to deal with too yesterday. She must have been thanking the gods we were on hand!

Mushi: But the man? Where is he? I have to see him to believe this!

Ash: He wasn't for hanging around.

Mushi: Where did he go?

Ash: Nineveh, apparently.

Mushi: Nineveh?! Out of the frying pan, into the fire!

Ash: That's exactly what I thought. Bit of a turnaround after heading west with you.

Mushi: Yeah. Bit of a turnaround ...

Jo Love, Spill the Beans

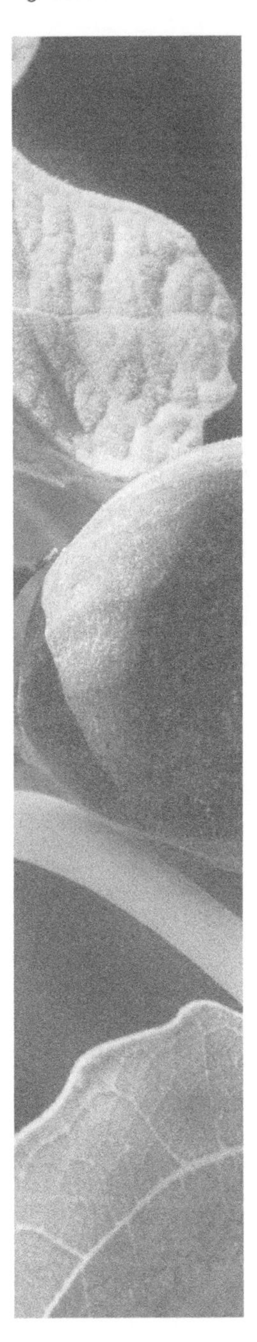

Something of a gourmet (Jonah 1–2)

I am considered something of a gourmet,
a gastronome,
in these parts.
I'm partial to a European
or a tasty Asian –
and I love Mediterranean.

My digestion is second to none –
I'm famous for it,
and I am always happy to experiment
with new tastes and textures,
refining my palate further.

But now I am somewhat nonplussed –
to put it mildly!
My lunch was, as I believed,
a tasty morsel from amongst the usual local snacks.
But, oh, the pain,
the chronic indigestion.
For three days I have groaned and rolled
and can bear it no longer.
I hear voices and am sorely undone.

I must head for the shore
and spew up this abominable thing,
this restless, noxious, indigestible,
endlessly fluttering dove,
and let it fly where it will, where it must …

Carolyn Morris

Note: Jonah means 'dove'.

Jonah rap (Jonah 1–4)

God said to Jonah, 'You're off to the big town
to tell the folk of Nineveh they've really let me down.
If they don't mend their ways real soon I'll punish them a lot:
so get your little rucksack on and set off at a trot.'

But Jonah said, 'No.' Jonah said, 'No.'
Jonah said, 'No', for he didn't want to go.

He set off west instead of east and took a boat to Spain,
because he heard the rain in Spain fell mainly on the plain;
he took his little rucksack off and used it as a pillow,
so he could hide from God and sleep while tossing on the billow.

For Jonah said, 'No' ...

The waves grew high, the lightning flashed; it poured and thunder roared;
the cargo ditched, the sailors yelled, 'There is a jinx on board!'
One minute Jonah in the hold was lying fast asleep,
next moment Jonah found himself a-sinking in the deep.

Cos Jonah said, 'No' ...

Just then God sent a rescuer, a big almighty whale.
It gave a gulp, took Jonah into shelter from the gale.
'Where am I?' wondered Jonah. 'I don't feel very well.
I don't think I'm in heaven and it's not hot enough for hell.'

Yes, Jonah said, 'No' ...

The whale swam on until it reached a gentle, sandy shore.
It gave a belch and Jonah landed on dry land once more.
'I should have known that God can see whatever wrong I do:
I'll have to go to Nineveh – and I've lost my rucksack too!'

For Jonah said, 'No' ...

At Nin'veh, Jonah's message was heard and understood:
The folk looked round and decided that they hadn't been very good.
'We'll change our ways and do God's will, no better folk he'll find.'
And God forgave, and Jonah learned that God can change his mind.

Then Jonah said, 'Yea.' Jonah said, 'Yea,'
for God's great mercy had won the day.

Marjory J.B. Williamson

Micah

Peace (Micah 4:1–4)

Peace.

Peace that is long enough
for the smith to beat weapons of war
into ploughshares
and pruning hooks.

Peace that is long enough
for our family to plant a vineyard
and for the grapes to ripen
and be trampled into wine.

Peace that is long enough
for us to plant fig trees
and to shelter beneath their branches
and enjoy their fruit.

Peace.
Hope.
No one afraid.

Our God has promised this.
We will worship him
and walk in his ways forever.

Ruth Burgess

Show love (Micah 6:8)

Show love,
act justly,
walk humbly with God:

enough challenge
and adventure

enough wonder
and creativity

enough tears
and laughter

enough task
for a lifetime;

enough company
and direction,
to see us safe home.

Ruth Burgess

We will look to You (Micah 7:7)

We will look to You, O God.
We will walk in Your ways.

We will live in peace.
We will not be afraid.

We will live in justice.
We will not lie or cheat.

We will speak for the poor.
We will speak against evil.

We will watch for You, O God.
We will wait and You will save us.

Ruth Burgess

Nahum

Nineveh has fallen (Nahum 1–3)

Emperor of Assyria,
Nineveh has fallen.

Chariots rush wildly through the streets.
The walls are down.

The gates by the river are broken.
The palace is in disarray.

The queen is taken.
Nineveh is destroyed.

Your people multiplied like insects;
you had more traders
than there are stars in the sky.

But now they have disappeared;
flown away like locusts,
and no one knows where they have gone.

Your governors are dead.
Your nobles are asleep forever.

Your people are scattered over the mountains.
There are no shepherds to bring them home.

Emperor of Assyria,
Nineveh has fallen.

The Lord God tolerates no rivals.
Nineveh is destroyed.

Ruth Burgess

Habakkuk

Climbing (Habakkuk 1:1–4, 2:1–4)

A monologue by the prophet Habakkuk. This could be read either before the Bible passage, or between Hab 2:1 and 2:2.

If all else fails, climb. Everything changes when I climb. I don't know why it makes a difference but it does. I never know what I expect to see, but nothing looks the same from somewhere higher. A hillside. A rooftop. A tree. A tower.

It is a hard place down there on the level. The level? That's the last word for it. Who would choose to live in these times? How did we allow this? Did we bring it on ourselves? Did we get complacent, faithless, proud?

When my neighbour goes to court, can he not expect a fair hearing any more? Is every judge corrupt? Has wealth become prized over compassion? Is violence now the answer to every disagreement? We are turning into our own oppressors, never mind the powers that threaten from Babylon. Who will be next to disappear from the streets? Whose child will be next to be orphaned? Which of us will survive, or will we be picked off one by one, two by two, enslaved and humiliated?

Yet God says nothing. God does nothing. Nothing changes.

But when I climb, everything changes. I have to come here. I have to just keep getting up to a higher place. How small the city is and how broad the land from here. I can see the fir tree and the stork living in harmony. The lions in all their wild energy do not turn on their own kind. The smell in the air is of flowers not fear. Here, heaven may remain silent, but the earth speaks. And the earth is still the Lord's.

Morning follows night and again I climb, and I stay here a while and I wait. Morning follows night and God takes no heed of my cries. How much longer? ...

Jo Love, Spill the Beans

Zephaniah

What's going to happen to Nineveh? (Zephaniah 2:13–15)

What, according to Zephaniah, will happen to Nineveh?

One thing is clear,
Nineveh will become a desert ruin.

But according to which translation of the Bible you consult,
an amazing variety of creatures
are going to take over the houses and streets.

According to the King James Version,
bitterns and cormorants will take up lodgings in the upper lintels,
and squawk out through the windows.

The Good News Bible has owls hooting in the darkness
and crows cawing on the doorsteps.

The Revised Standard Version introduces vultures and ravens,
and a hedgehog snuffling underneath the floor.

The Message has racoons and coyotes
bedding down happily in the basement.

The Jerusalem Bible goes for porcupines
who apparently nest round the cornices at night.

The Wycliffe Bible has an onocrotalus and an urchin in the doorway;
according to my dictionary that's a great white pelican
and maybe an elf or a sprite.

The Easy to Read Bible goes for blackbirds.

The International Children's Bible has sheep and goats.

What, according to Zephaniah, will happen to Nineveh?

One thing is clear –
it's going to be a very interesting place!

Ruth Burgess

It's coming (Zephaniah 3:14–20)

It's coming!
I promise you the time is coming.
I will bring your scattered people home.

I will delight in you.
I will sing to you.
I will give you new life.

You will be poor,
but you will prosper,
you will be secure.

You will know my name
and you will trust me.
No one will make you afraid.

It's coming!
I promise you the time is coming.
I will bring your scattered people home.

Ruth Burgess

Haggai

I am going to shake things up (Haggai 1–2)

I will be with you. This is my promise.
I will always be with you. Don't be afraid.

For now you struggle.
You never have enough food, wine and clothing.
But it will change.

Peace and prosperity will come.
I am going to shake things up.
I am going to turn everything upside down.

I keep my promises.
Don't be afraid.

Ruth Burgess

Good news and bad news (Haggai 2:1–9)

Haggai was a wise old man, the last of his generation. He was like a grandfather to the people, and when he spoke they all knew it would be good, because Haggai wasn't just old and wise, he was also a man who heard from God.

The people were sad. So many of their friends had moved away, and all the good things were just memories. It seemed like nothing good was ever going to happen again.

Then Haggai called them all together, everyone, even Zerubbabel the Governor, and Joshua who was the High Priest's son. Everyone who was anyone came when Haggai called.

'I've got a new message!' he shouted. 'I've got good news and bad news.'

'God says this: "There are going to be more difficult times ahead, but be strong! All of you, be strong: yes, you, Zerubbabel, and you, Joshua. Every last one of you: be strong! Because soon, very soon, it will all be good again. In fact, it will be better than good – it will be brilliant!"'

Julie Rennick, Spill the Beans

Zechariah

Now you can stand (Zechariah 3)

Even if you are standing before the angel of the Lord,
the tempter is still at your side.
He wants to point out your failings, your sins.

Have you got a hope?
Can you cast off your filthy clothes,
your filthy past?
Can you be made new?

Yes, yes and yes!
The fire from which you were rescued
has cleansed you,
and the transformation is made complete
as you are tenderly clothed
in a pristine turban and fresh garments.

Now you can stand before the angel of the Lord
ready to walk in the way of the Lord.
Until when?
Until the day when the Messiah comes.

Pam Hathorn

The faithful city (Zechariah 8)

Leader: God gave this message to Zechariah:

A: I have longed to help Jerusalem
because of my deep love for her people.

B: I will return to Jerusalem and live there:
it will be known as the faithful city.

A: Once again old men and women,
so old that they use a stick when they walk,
will be sitting in the city squares.

B: Once again the streets will be full
of boys and girls playing.

A: People will sow their crops in peace;
the vines will bear grapes.

B: The earth will produce food;
there will be plenty of rain.

Leader: These are the things you must do:

A: Speak the truth to one another.

B: In the courts practise real justice,
the kind that brings peace.

A: Do not plan ways to hurt each other.

B: Do not tell lies about each other.

Leader: Have courage.
Do not be afraid.
You must love truth and love peace.

Ruth Burgess

Malachi

We prepare the way (Malachi 3:1)

See, I am sending my messenger to prepare the way before me, and the Lord whom you seek will suddenly come to his temple. The messenger of the covenant in whom you delight – indeed he is coming, says the Lord of hosts. (Mal 3:1, NRSV)

When we record
a book for someone with
macular degeneration;
where we recycle hearing aids
for folk we'll never
meet;

whenever we spend our
days off transporting
rescued animals
to their forever homes;

wherever we speak words
of welcome and not
turn our backs,

we prepare the way
to you for others.

Thom M Shuman

God loves us (Malachi 3:1–6)

God loves us
and we have messed up.

We are cheats.
We have cheated our neighbours.
We have cheated those who are vulnerable.
We have cheated strangers.
We have cheated God.

God's messenger is coming
and he will see through us.
With strong soap
he will scrub us clean.
With a smith's white-hot fire
he will refine us,
the evil in us will be burnt away.

God loves us.
God does not stop loving us.
God does not change.
But we need to.

Ruth Burgess

Tobit

The story of Tobit and his family (Tobit 1–14)

When I met them I called myself Azarias. I'd been watching them for a long time. They were good people.

Tobit was an old man now, and he was blind and poor. But I had watched him over the years. He had kept the commandments. He prayed, he tithed his crops, he had been generous to his neighbours. He had faithfully buried the bodies of the dead. Tobit was married to Anna, a weaver, a good hard-working woman, and they had one son called Tobias, not yet betrothed.

Then there was Sarah, a young woman, the daughter of Raguel and his wife, Edna. Sarah longed to settle down and have children. She had already been married seven times and each time an evil demon who lived in her house had killed her new husband on their wedding night. She was often very sad and she prayed to God in her despair.

I had watched over them. I had brought their prayers into God's presence. It was now time to act.

Tobit had remembered that he had left some money with a relative who lived in a town a few days' journey away. He had asked Tobias to collect the money. But it was a dangerous journey and Tobias would need a companion, and so I offered to be that companion. Tobit questioned me, and decided that I was a distant relative and a good journeying companion for his son.

As we got ready to leave, Anna began to cry. Tobias was their only son. She was afraid that something would happen to us on the journey. Tobias kissed his mother and father goodbye and Tobit wished us a safe journey. He told Anna not to worry, an angel would look after us. An angel was closer than they knew.

So Tobias and I set off, and Tobias' dog came with us. I was glad. I like dogs. We walked all day, and at sunset we camped by the river. Tobias had gone to wash his feet when suddenly a big fish leapt out of the river and began to nibble his toes. He yelled! I shouted to him to grab the fish and he did, and dragged it up onto the riverbank.

I told Tobias to cut the fish open and to take out the gall bladder and the heart and the liver and to keep them. Then we cooked the fish and ate some of it for our supper. It was good. The dog enjoyed it too. We salted what was left over and took it with us on our journey.

The next day, while we were travelling, Tobias asked me why we had kept the fish's gall bladder and heart and liver. I told him that if you burn the heart and the liver of a fish in a house where a demon is living, the smell will drive it away and it will never come back. Tobias asked about the gall bladder, and I told him that if you rubbed it on the eyes of someone who is blind, and then blew into their eyes, they would be able to see again. Tobias was impressed.

When we were getting near to the town I told Tobias that we would stay with Raguel and Edna and Sarah that night, as they were our relatives. And I told him about Sarah, how she was brave and beautiful and how her father was rich. I then told him that Sarah would make him a good wife, and that I would discuss the matter with Raguel. Then they could get married and we would take Sarah back with us to Tobit and Anna.

But someone had told Tobias the story of Sarah and her seven dead husbands, and he wasn't very keen on the idea! But I reminded him of the fish's heart and liver, and I told him again what to do with it.

We found Raguel's house and the family welcomed us. Raguel told Tobias how much he looked like Tobit. I talked with Raguel and he was happy for Tobias to marry Sarah. And Raguel wrote out a marriage contract for them and blessed them. We ate well that night – a marriage feast.

After the meal Edna took Sarah up to the bedroom to wait for Tobias. Sarah began to cry, but Edna wiped her tears away and told her that she was sure that this time God would look after her and make her happy.

Later Raguel and Edna took Tobias up to Sarah's bedroom. He had remembered what I had told him and he took the fish's heart and liver with him. Sarah watched him as he put the heart and liver on some burning incense. The smell drove the demon far, far away and I made sure that it never came back.

Sarah and Tobias prayed and asked God to look after them and bless their marriage. They prayed that they would live long and grow old together. Then they slept.

Later that night Raguel called his servants together. They went out to dig a grave. He was afraid that in the morning Tobias would be dead. Before dawn he asked his wife to send a servant to see if Tobias was alive. The servant looked into the bedroom and saw Tobias and Sarah fast asleep. Raguel was overjoyed and he ordered his servants to fill the grave up again and to do it before breakfast!

The next day Raguel called for Tobias and told him that he would not let us go home until they had spent two weeks feasting with friends and family. He also told Tobias that he would give him and Sarah half of what he owned to take back with them to Tobit and Anna.

While this was happening I went to the house of the relative who had been looking after Tobit's money and I collected it for him.

At last we were ready to travel. Tobias was eager to get going; he knew that his parents would be worried about him. With us we were taking servants, sheep, cattle, clothes and furniture. And bags of money and some donkeys and camels. It was going to be a long journey. The dog made itself very useful by looking after the sheep.

Raguel hugged Tobias and asked God to bless him and Sarah. Edna kissed them both and sent us safely on our way.

Tobias was right about Tobit and Anna. They were worried. We should have been home days ago. I knew that Anna took herself out on the road each day to watch for us. I told Tobias that he should go on ahead of us, and to remember to take the fish's gall bladder with him. So he went on ahead and his dog went with him. When Anna saw him she ran back to Tobit to tell him that Tobias was coming. As Tobit stumbled through the gate of their courtyard Tobias caught him and he rubbed the gall bladder on Tobit's eyes as I had told him to.

Tobit threw his arms around Tobias' neck and wept for joy. He could see him. He could see again.

They came together to the city gates to welcome Sarah and the rest of us. And Tobit blessed Sarah as he led her to her new home.

When they had feasted Tobit called Tobias and told him that he should pay me well for our journey. And Tobias called me and told me that he was going to give me half of what we had brought back with us from Sarah's house. He, like his father, was a good and generous man.

I decided that it was time to come clean. I took them aside and I told them who I was. I told them how I had watched over them for a long time and how I had taken their prayers and Sarah's prayers to God.

'I am Raphael,' I told them. 'I am one of seven angels who are close to God, always ready to serve him.' They were very frightened, but I told them not to be, that God had wanted me to help them and had always been close to us.

And then I left them. They could no longer see me. And they sang and sang and they praised God. And the dog joined in and barked.

Ruth Burgess

Journey well (Tobit 5:21)

Journey well.
May good angels go with you.
May your journey be fruitful.
May you return home safe and sound.

Ruth Burgess

Let us grow old together (Tobit 8:4–9)

God we praise you.
We honour your name forever.

You made everything in heaven.
You created all the creatures of the earth.

You made Adam.
You created Eve to be his wife.

We are in love with each other.
We want to support each other.

We want to have children.
We want to share each other's lives.

Be kind to us.
Let us grow old together.

Hear our prayers, God.
Amen
Amen

Ruth Burgess

Judith

Judith and Holofernes (Judith 8–15)

Judith: An Israelite widow
Keziah: Judith's servant
Uzziah: A town elder
A captain: An Assyrian patrol
Holofernes: General of the Assyrian armies
Bagoas: Assistant to Holofernes
Achior: General of the Ammonites
Narrator

Keziah: Judith? Mistress?

Judith: Keziah – have you managed to find out what all the shouting was about?

Keziah: Yes. I'm afraid it's bad news. You know it's been so long since the Assyrian army cut us off from our water supply ...

Judith: Thirty-four days. I've been keeping count.

Keziah: And even with the rationing, the cisterns are all running dry now. If it would only rain we might refill them, but nobody dares go down to the springs for fear of the Assyrians.

Judith: We've been careful here, but even so, our great cisterns are almost empty.

Keziah: Well, the people are getting desperate. So this morning they mobbed the City Fathers and blamed them for not making peace with the Assyrians. They said they'd rather be slaves than watch their wives and children die of thirst. They demanded that Uzziah and the others hand the whole city over to this General Holofernes straight away.

Judith: And what did they say?

Keziah: Uzziah told them to be brave for five more days. Then he promised that if God didn't save us within those five days, he'd do what they asked.

Judith: He promised what?! Keziah, go and fetch the City Fathers here. I need a word with them!

Narrator: Judith's maid went up into the city and came back with Uzziah, the governing elder, and his two colleagues.

Judith: You have to listen to me, gentlemen. This promise you've given today, it's not right. You may be in charge of this city – but who are you to tell God how quickly he has to act?

Uzziah: Now, dear, I know you've done a grand job of managing your husband's estate ever since he died and left you a widow, but this is politics.

Judith: It's a matter of faith. Don't try to tie God down. It won't do any good to threaten God, or to argue with him. We are waiting for him to intervene – wouldn't it be better to call upon him to help us? He'll hear us if it pleases him. Round here we've only ever worshipped God. We haven't offended him with idols like our ancestors did. Let's thank him for putting us to the test, not try to test him.

Uzziah: I couldn't agree more, my dear. Everyone knows you have great wisdom. But there was no alternative. The people are very thirsty, and they made us take an oath, and we can't break a solemn oath. Now, you're a devout woman. You pray to God to send us rain to fill our cisterns. That's the answer.

Judith: I shall do something, I promise you. Stand at the city gate tonight, and I shall go out with my maid. Within your precious five days you'll see what God will do through me.

Uzziah: Go in peace, then, and may the Lord God go before you to take revenge on our enemies.

Narrator: That evening, at the very time when the evening incense was being offered in the Temple at Jerusalem, Judith cried out to God for guidance.

Judith: Lord my God, you inspired my forefather Simeon to use cunning and the sword to avenge a great wrong. O God, my God, hear me too. Your power doesn't depend on numbers or weapons, for you are the God of the lowly, the helper of the oppressed, upholder of the weak and saviour of those without hope. Help me now to bring down the pride of these Assyrians before they destroy your people and defile your holy sanctuary. Crush them by the hand of a woman. And I've always been a truthful person, so please help me to lie convincingly just this once.

Keziah: Are you planning to take a sword, mistress? I'm not sure we've got one in the house.

Judith: No, we won't need to take a sword with us. Help me take off this sackcloth. I'll need a bath, and some proper perfumed oil, and get out my finest robes and my best special-occasion sandals. Anklets, bracelets, rings, earrings, ornaments, tiara, you know the routine.

Keziah: I'd almost forgotten, it's been so long. You do have some lovely things, mistress.

Narrator: When Judith was arrayed at her most drop-dead gorgeous, she handed her maid a big bag to carry.

Keziah: What's in here, mistress? Some kind of weapon, I suppose.

Judith: No, there's a bottle of wine, a bottle of oil, parched grain, dried fruit and some pretty fine bread. And the cooking pots, of course.

Keziah: Of course ... What are we going to do with those?

Judith: Wait and see.

Narrator: Judith and her maid went out to the city gate. Uzziah and the other city elders were standing there waiting for her.

Uzziah: Wow – what a difference! You look stunning! Er, may the God of our fathers grant you favour and fulfil your plans, to the glory of Israel.

Judith: Praise and glory be to the Lord my God! Order the city gates to be opened for me, and I will go and deal with those problems you told me about.

Narrator: So the young men opened the city gates to let Judith and her maid go out. The men of the city watched her all the way down the mountain and along the valley until she was out of sight. As the two women went on through the valley, they met an Assyrian patrol.

Captain: You there! Who are you, and where have you come from, and where are you off to?

Judith: I am a daughter of the Hebrews, but I'm running away because they are about to be given over to you and exterminated. I want to see Holofernes your commander. I'll show him how he can capture the whole hill country without losing a single soldier.

Captain: Smart move, gorgeous. We'll give you an escort to the general's tent. Don't be afraid when you see him, just tell him what you've told us. He'll see you right.

Narrator: A hundred Assyrian soldiers were sent to escort Judith to Holofernes' tent. Sensation in the camp! Quite a crowd gathered around while she was waiting to be let in, and many were the admiring comments and wolf whistles. Then a horde of staff officers and servants came out to conduct her into the tent. Holofernes was relaxing on his bed under a canopy woven with purple and gold and decorated with emeralds and precious stones, but when they told him about Judith he soon sprang up and went to greet her. Judith prostrated herself before him, in the best court manner, and his slaves raised her up.

Holofernes: Well, woman, you've nothing to fear now you've come to me. I've never hurt anyone who chose to serve Nebuchadnezzar, King of all the world. I wouldn't have lifted a spear against your people if they hadn't insulted me. This is all their fault.

Judith: O my lord, all the world knows your wisdom and skill, and that all men serve Nebuchadnezzar the king because of you. Now if you will follow the advice of your humble maidservant, God has sent me to you with information that will let you astonish the whole world by your achievement. You know that Achior the commander of the Ammonites told you our God will defend his people against any force?

Holofernes: He had a lot to say on that subject. Until I had him tied up and handed over to join your people under siege.

Judith: I've heard him. But now my people are about to commit a sin that will enrage God and cause their total destruction. Your blockade has them in so much trouble that they have almost no food and water left. Now they propose to slaughter their cattle and eat all the parts that they should dedicate to God. They even plan to eat the first fruits of wine and oil which they have already solemnly presented to God. They've sent to Jerusalem for permission, and when the permission arrives they will give God this mortal insult, and God will hand them over to you to be destroyed.

Holofernes: You interest me greatly.

Judith: Naturally, when I heard all this I fled from the city. Your maid-servant is a woman of faith, and serves the God of heaven by day and by night. I'll stay here with you, and every night I'll go out into the valley and pray to God, and God will tell me when the people have committed this sin. Then I'll come and tell you, and your army will be able to wipe them out without resistance; and I'll take you on to conquer Jerusalem, and you will lead them like sheep that have no shepherd, and not a dog will so much as open its mouth to growl at you. God has told me this, and sent me to tell you.

Holofernes: Your god has done well, to bring destruction on those who have insulted the Great King. You are not only beautiful, but wise with it. If you do as you've promised, your god shall be my god, and you shall have a place in King Nebuchadnezzar's palace as a real celebrity. Now my servants will set you a feast with my own finest food and wine.

Judith:	Oh no, my lord, I can't eat anything that might offend God. Please don't trouble about me, I've brought my own supplies.
Holofernes:	Where can my servants get more of this food for you when yours runs out?
Judith:	That won't be a problem. I won't have used up what I've brought with me before the Lord carries out what he plans to do by my hand.
Narrator:	For the next three nights Judith slept in the tent where Holofernes kept his valuables. Every night she arose before dawn and was permitted to go out of the camp to pray. Every night she went to the spring and washed herself clean before praying to God to show her how she could save her people. Then she went back to the tent and kept herself pure, until she ate her food towards evening. On the fourth night, Holofernes decided to throw a party. He didn't invite any of his officers. Instead he said to Bagoas, the eunuch who was his personal assistant:
Holofernes:	Go and tell that Hebrew woman you've been looking after to come and eat and drink with us. I'll be disgraced forever if I don't give her what she's been waiting for – she'll laugh at us.
Narrator:	The eunuch very politely invited Judith to come and enjoy herself with Holofernes and his servants.
Bagoas:	This beautiful maidservant will please come to my lord and be favoured in his presence, and drink wine and be merry with us, and

be like one of the daughters of the Assyrians who serve the great King Nebuchadnezzar.

Judith: Who am I to refuse my lord? It will be a great honour for me – a joy to remember until the day I die.

Narrator: So she dressed herself in all her finery, and her maid went into Holofernes' own tent and spread soft fleeces for Judith to recline on. Then Judith came in and lay down, and Holofernes could hardly wait.

Holofernes: Drink now, and be merry with us!

Judith: I will gladly drink with my lord. This is the greatest day of my life.

Narrator: But what she ate and drank was the food and wine her maid brought her. Holofernes didn't care. He was so excited that he drank more wine than he'd ever had at one sitting before, and by the time his servants tactfully went off to bed, he had so much wine in him that as soon as he lay down on his bed he passed out. When everything was quiet, Judith stood beside the bed and prayed very hard. Then she went to the bedpost by Holofernes' head, and took down his sword which was hanging there. She seized Holofernes by his hair.

Judith: Give me strength this day, O Lord God of Israel!

Narrator: And with two mighty blows, she chopped off his head. Then she rolled his body onto the floor and took down the beautiful embroidered bed canopy with all its jewels. After a moment she went out and gave his head to her maid, who put it in the food bag. Then the two of them went quietly out of the camp, at their usual hour of prayer. But this time they went on past the spring and up to the gates of the city.

Judith: Open, open the gates! God, our God is still with us and his power has saved us from our enemies!

Narrator: The men of the city rushed down to the city gates calling for Uzziah and the other elders.

Uzziah: Judith? Did you say Judith is back? But how can she have survived?

Narrator: They opened the gates, and Judith and her maid came in.

Judith: Praise God, oh praise him! Praise God, for he has destroyed our enemies by my hand this very night!

Uzziah: But ... how did you escape from General Holofernes?

Judith: I put his head in a bag.

Uzziah: You put his head in a bag ... that bag?

Judith: Look!

Uzziah: General Achior, you've been in the presence of the Assyrian commander. Is that ...?

Achior: I warned him. I said, 'Pass them by, my lord, because their God will defend and protect them, and we shall be put to shame before the whole world.' Yes, that's Holofernes. And that embroidered canopy was hanging above his bed the last time I saw it.

Uzziah: O daughter, you are blessed by the Most High God above all women on earth. Your hope will never depart from the hearts of men, as they remember the power of God. Blessed are you, Lord our God, King of all the earth, who have delivered us from our enemies by the hand of this your servant!

Achior: I'm convinced. Your God is the true God. I wish to be circumcised and belong to the House of Israel forever.

Narrator: At dawn they hung Holofernes' head on the city wall, and all the fighting men took up their weapons and went out to the mountain passes. The Assyrians saw them, and the other commanders sent Holofernes' personal assistant to wake him up in a hurry.

Bagoas: Pardon this intrusion, my lord, but ... Oh! Oh no! The slaves have tricked us! That Hebrew woman has brought disaster on us all! For look: here is my lord Holofernes on the ground, and his head is not on him!

Narrator: The whole Assyrian army panicked and fled, hotly pursued by the Israelites. All through the hill country more Israelites grabbed up their weapons and joined in the hunt, and they chased the Assyrians back through Gilead and Galilee, even beyond Damascus and its borders. Then came the looting of the Assyrians' abandoned camp, and the celebrations, the songs of thanksgiving and the dancing. Judith received a great many proposals of marriage, but she turned them all down. She became more and more famous, and grew old caring for her dead husband's estate, until she died at the age of one hundred and five. And no one ever again spread terror among the people of Israel in the days of Judith, or for a long time after her death.

Liz Varley

The Wisdom of Solomon

Like everyone else (Wisdom 7:1–6)

Like every human being, I am mortal.

I am a descendant of the first human being
who was made from the soil and God's breath.

During the pleasure of intercourse I was conceived
from the seed of a man and the egg of a woman,
and I grew in my mother's womb.

When I was born I came into the world like everyone else.
I began to breathe the air everyone breathes
and my first sound, like your first sound,
was a cry.

I was wrapped up in cloths and cared for.

No one, not even a queen or a king, had a different beginning.
For all of us there is one way into life,
and for all of us there will be one way out.

Ruth Burgess

What's Wisdom like? (Wisdom 7:21b–8:1)

What's Wisdom like?

Wisdom is feminine.
Wisdom is a she.

She is the breath of God's power.
She is the mirror of God's activity,
an image of God's goodness.

She's dependable, she's confident.
She is intelligent, she's kind.
She is more beautiful than the sun and stars.
She is bright light.

She seeks out those who are honest and holy
and makes of them God's friends and messengers.

God loves those in whom Wisdom has made her home.

Ruth Burgess

Ecclesiasticus

How to behave at a dinner party (Ecclesiasticus 31:12–32:11)

Number one:
as you come in
don't say:
'Wow! Look at all that food!'
That's not polite.

Number two:
don't reach out for everything you fancy

and

Number three:
definitely don't elbow people out of the way
so that you can reach the food you like.

Number four:
don't get into a contest
to prove how much you can drink.
Nobody respects a drunken fool.

Number five:
enjoy the conversation around you,
don't say too much yourself
and listen respectfully to other people's stories.

Number six:
leave the party at the right time,
don't be the last to go.

And lastly
number seven:
don't forget to thank God (and your host)
for a great night.

Ruth Burgess

The workers (Ecclesiasticus 38:1–34)

Give doctors the respect they deserve.
Give thanks for those who mix medicines.
Give a scholar time to study.

Thank a farmhand for the skill to plough a straight furrow
and his love for the animals he feeds.

Artists and craftspeople take time to produce new designs.
They work into the night to finish their work.
The blacksmith shapes iron on the anvil,
the potter works clay on the wheel.

All these people are skilled with their hands,
each one an expert at their craft.
Their work holds this world together.
Their work is their offering, their prayer.

Ruth Burgess

Susanna

She was beautiful (Susanna 1-64)

She was beautiful. She was deeply religious. She was married to Joakim. Her name was Susanna.

There were two older men who fancied her, lusted over her, the story says. Both were judges. They were so obsessed with her that they lost the desire to work or pray.

Neither judge told the other how he felt, until one day, trying to catch a glimpse of Susanna, they met each other and told each other their feelings. After that they watched together, hoping to see Susanna on her own.

One day Susanna went into Joakim's garden, unaware that the two men were secretly watching her. It was a hot day and Susanna decided to have a bath. Her servants locked the garden gates and went to fetch her oil and perfume.

As the servants left, the two men came out of hiding. They told Susanna that unless she had sex with them, they would declare in court that she had sent her servants away so that she could have sex with a young man.

Susanna refused to give in to them and began to scream. When her servants came running the two men told their story of a young man in the garden and the servants were shocked and ashamed.

The next day the two judges sent for Susanna. She came to court with all her family. She was so graceful and beautiful that the two judges ordered her to remove her veil so that they could enjoy looking at her. Then the two judges told their story. They said that there had been a young man hidden in the garden and that they had caught him lying with Susanna. Because he was strong, they could not hold him, and he had opened the garden gates and run away.

The people believed the judges and Susanna was condemned to death.

Susanna prayed to God to save her, and God heard her, and sent a wise man called Daniel to the court. Daniel, on hearing the facts, quickly realised that there was little substance to the judges' story, and he asked for the two judges to be separated.

Daniel asked the first judge under what kind of tree had he seen the young man lying with Susanna, and he answered 'under a mastic tree'. When Daniel asked the second judge the same question, the man answered, 'under an evergreen oak'.

The people realised that the judges had been lying and turned against them. Susanna was freed and the two judges were put to death.

After this Daniel was held in high regard by the people. They recognised that his wisdom came from God.

Ruth Burgess

Bel and the Dragon

Daniel and the priests of Bel (Bel and the Dragon 1–22)

Long ago in the land of Babylon the people worshipped an idol called Bel. Bel was made of clay covered with bronze and was placed in a temple that was run by a group of priests. Every day the people took an offering to Bel: an offering of 720 pounds of flour, 50 gallons of wine and 40 sheep.

One day King Cyrus asked Daniel, who was an Israelite, why he didn't go to the temple to worship Bel. Daniel explained to him that he worshipped the living God, who made heaven and earth. The king asked Daniel if he didn't believe that Bel was a living god – after all Bel ate and drank the offerings made to him every day.

Daniel laughed and told the king that he was being fooled: Bel had never eaten or drunk anything – he was just a statue of clay. The king was angry and he called together the 70 priests of Bel and told them what Daniel had said. Then he asked the priests to prove to him that Bel did eat and drink the offerings. If they could prove it he would have Daniel put to death for insulting Bel. If they could not prove it, they would be killed.

The priests took Daniel and the king into the temple and placed the food and wine on a table. They told the king that after he and Daniel left the temple the king should lock the doors and put his royal seal on the lock. The temple would be locked all night and not opened until the next morning.

After the priests had left the temple the king checked that all the wine and food was on the table in front of the statue of Bel, ready for the god to eat and drink. Then Daniel fetched his servants and ordered them to scatter ashes all over the temple floor. Then the king and Daniel and his servants left the temple and the king locked and sealed the door.

That night the 70 priests, with their wives and children, entered the temple by a secret entrance, as they usually did, and ate all the food and drank the wine.

Early the next morning the king and Daniel went to the temple of Bel. The seals on the door had not been broken. As soon as they opened the door the king looked in and saw the empty table in front of the statue of Bel, and he shouted: 'You are great, Bel! You really are a god!'

But Daniel began to laugh and said to the king, 'Before you go in, look at the floor and tell me whose footprints you see there.' The king looked and the floor was covered in footprints, footprints of women and children and men.

The king quickly had the priests and their families arrested and brought to the temple. The priests showed him the secret passages and doors through which they had entered the temple each night to eat and drink the people's offerings to Bel.

And Cyrus the king was so angry that he had the priests put to death, and he gave the statue of Bel to Daniel.

Daniel broke the idol into little pieces and he and his servants tore down its temple.

Ruth Burgess

Five ways to dispose of a dragon (Bel and the Dragon 23–27)

1. Find a knight in shining armour who will slay the dragon for you. This method is particularly effective if beautiful maidens are also present.

2. Swoop down on your broomstick and cast a disappearing spell on the dragon. This method only works if you can do magic.

3. Find a new home for the dragon and persuade it to go there. This method only works if you can speak dragon.

4. Give the dragon lots of treasure if it will move home. This method only works if you can speak dragon and are rich.

5. Get together an army to fight the dragon. This method only works if you can persuade enough people to join your army.

If none of these methods work you could try Daniel's method:

Daniel was an Israelite living in Babylon. The people of Babylon worshipped a huge dragon and they thought this dragon was a god. Daniel went to King Cyrus, the king of Babylon, and asked him for permission to kill the dragon. He told Cyrus that he could kill the dragon without using a club or a sword. King Cyrus gave his permission – he did not think it was possible to kill the dragon because he thought the dragon was a god.

Daniel knew that dragons are usually hungry and that they will eat almost anything, although tender young maidens, especially beautiful ones, are the ultimate dragon treat. But Daniel's method did not require young maidens, or magic spells or even weapons. Daniel's method to dispose of the dragon required the ability to make cakes!

Daniel's dragon-disposal cakes were special. First of all he took some barrels of tar and boiled it until it was runny, then he stirred in pounds and pounds of fat, and kept stirring until it had dissolved, and then he added lots of fur and hair to help bind the mixture together. Daniel boiled the mixture for a long time, until it was nearly solid, and then he let it cool a little and shaped it into cakes – lots and lots and lots of cakes.

Daniel offered some cakes to the dragon and it ate them. The dragon looked at Daniel expectantly and Daniel fed it a few more cakes, and then a few more, and then a lot more. Soon the dragon's belly was getting bigger and bigger as it ate more and more and more cakes. Daniel did not know how many cakes the dragon could eat, but he'd made loads. And the dragon went on eating more and more and more cakes. It was as if it couldn't stop. It ate more and more and more and more cakes ...... and then the dragon burst!

End of dragon. Good method, Daniel. Thank you for the recipe. If we ever need to dispose of a dragon we'll know what to do.

Ruth Burgess

Into the lions' den (Bel and the Dragon 28–42)

Scene 1: The king's court

A mob is shouting and screaming at the king. Daniel is beside the throne with several guards next to him.

Mob: You have become a Jew!
You have killed Bel.
You have killed the priests.
You have killed the dragon.
The king looks fearful and cowers on his throne.

King: I ... I ...

Mob: You are a puppet of Daniel.
He whispers in your ear.
We have lost our living
and all that we hold dear!
We had a golden God.
We had our precious Bel.
But in your stupid tyranny
you condemned our god to Hell.
We had another great god,
the dragon god so fierce.
You couldn't keep him safe –
with a spear you did him pierce!

King: No! No! No!
Daniel used no spear.
He used no hefty club.
The dragon ate a tasty snack of
tar and hair and fat.
He gobbled it.
He chewed it.
He crunched it and he munched it.
And sadly that was that!

Mob: Hand Daniel over to us!
Bring him here –
bring him now!
For if you don't
there'll be a terrible row.
And you we will destroy.
We will remove you from this place,
no more to see your face!
Hand Daniel over to us!
Hand him to us now!

The king reluctantly signals to his guards to hand Daniel over. The mob pull Daniel this way and that, pushing and jabbing him.

Mob: So, Bane of Gods, we have you.
Dragon-slayer we have you.
Whisperer, magician, foreigner and Jew!
The lions we have starved for days.
No humans, sheep, no meat to eat.
Seven lions that are hungry –
into their den you'll go.
And they will chew you through.
And they will chew you through.

The mob manhandles Daniel out of the court.

Scene 2

A simple room. A large pot of steaming stew is on the table and a tall bearded man is breaking bread into the pot. A bright light shines and then an angel appears.

Angel: Habbakuk!

Habbakuk: Yes, that is me, prophet of the most high God.

Angel: That food, who is it for?

Habbakuk: It is for the reapers in the field.

Angel: It smells very good.

Habbakuk: Thank you. They have worked very hard today.

Angel: You are an honourable servant of God and of his people.

Habbakuk: Thank you! This is a good day. The reaping is almost done and I have not burned the meat for once!

Angel: Take the food that you have to Babylon, to Daniel, in the lions' den.

Habbakuk: Sir, I have never seen Babylon and I know nothing about a lions' den.

The angel 'grabs' Habbakuk by the hair. Habbakuk grabs the pot and they whirl off. The stage darkens. There are flashes of light and the sound of a great wind.

Scene 3: The lions' den

As the lights go up Habbakuk and the angel are standing directly at the entrance to the lions' den. Daniel is sitting inside surrounded by seven lions, who are behaving like domestic cats (have people dressed up in lion onesies). One is resting its head in his lap as he strokes it.

Habbakuk: Daniel! Take this food that God has sent you. Take it quickly now.

Daniel: You have remembered me, O God, and have not forsaken those who love you. I thank you, my brother.

Habbakuk: All in a day's work for a prophet.

Habbakuk spies the angel approaching with outstretched hand.

But I am not too enamoured with this method of transport –

The angel 'grabs' his hair again and they whirl away as before.

Stage darkens. Then lights come back on.

Daniel finishes eating his food, sharing some with the lions; and then lies back on one of the lions, who purrs contentedly.

Scene 4: The next morning, outside the lions' den

The king, dressed in mourning, comes to pay his respects to Daniel, who he knows must be completely eaten by the lions. He peers into the den and sees that Daniel is alive.

King: You are great, O Lord, the God of Daniel, and there is no other besides you!

He pulls Daniel out and embraces him. As they leave the stage he shouts:

Guards, arrest that mob and feed them to the lions!

At once the lions remember how hungry they are and begin to prowl. A struggling group of people are thrown by the guards into the den. Appropriate noises are made by the mob and lions as the lights go out.

Constantina Alexander

2 Maccabees

Editing is not easy (2 Maccabees 2:19–32)

Jason of Cyrene
was a great historian;
his books were accurate
and full of detail.

Jason of Cyrene
told the story of Judas Maccabaeus
and his brothers in five volumes.
Sadly, not everyone has time
to read five books.

My readers want brevity,
they do not want detail.
From Jason's five books
I need to edit it down to one!

Editing is not easy;
it requires much concentration.
I will need to burn
the midnight oil.

Editing is complicated;
you cannot please everyone –
it is like trying to
prepare a banquet
for people
who have very different tastes.

Yours was the whole picture,
the detailed master plan.
I am akin to a painter and decorator,
making your work beautiful,
attractive to your readers.

Enough from the editor.
If I am not careful
my long introduction
will mean that the story itself
will need to be even shorter.

Jason of Cyrene,
I will do my best.

Ruth Burgess

Sources and acknowledgements

'I said no (Esther 1)' – by Ruth Burgess, from *Acorns and Archangels: Resources for Ordinary Time – Feast of the Transfiguration to All Hallows'*, Ruth Burgess (Ed.), Wild Goose Publications, 2009

'God's glory (Psalm 19:1–6)' – by Ruth Burgess, from *Iona Abbey Worship Book*, Iona Community, Wild Goose Publications, 2017

'God tells us how to behave (Psalm 19:7–11,14)' – by Ruth Burgess, from *Iona Abbey Worship Book*, Iona Community, Wild Goose Publications, 2017

'God you are big and strong (Psalm 104)' – by Ruth Burgess, from *Iona Abbey Worship Book*, Iona Community, Wild Goose Publications, 2017

'Where does our help come from? (Psalm 121)' – by Ruth Burgess from *Iona Abbey Worship Book*, Iona Community, Wild Goose Publications, 2017

'You know me, God (Psalm 139)' – by Ruth Burgess, from *Iona Abbey Worship Book*, Iona Community, Wild Goose Publications, 2017

'It is good to sing (Psalm 147)' – by Ruth Burgess, from *Iona Abbey Worship Book*, Iona Community, Wild Goose Publications, 2017

'Wisdom is shouting out (Proverbs 8:1–12,18–21)' first written for Christian Aid, 2018

'You were there (Proverbs 8:22–30)' – by Ruth Burgess, from *Acorns and Archangels: Resources for Ordinary Time – Feast of the Transfiguration to All Hallows'*, Ruth Burgess (Ed.), Wild Goose Publications, 2009

'One day (Jonah 1–4)' – by Christopher, from *Acorns and Archangels: Resources for Ordinary Time – Feast of the Transfiguration to All Hallows'*, Ruth Burgess (Ed.), Wild Goose Publications, 2009

'Show love (Micah 6:8)' – by Ruth Burgess, from *Acorns and Archangels: Resources for Ordinary Time – Feast of the Transfiguration to All Hallows'*, Ruth Burgess (Ed.), Wild Goose Publications, 2009

Spill the Beans material © the contributors. Spill the Beans is 'a lectionary-based resource with a Scottish flavour for Sunday Schools, Junior Churches and worship leaders': http://spillbeans.org.uk/

About the contributors

Sarah Agnew is a storyteller, poet and minister. She serves in the Canberra Central Uniting Church Parish in Australia. For more of her work, see: praythestory.blogspot.com and sarahtellsstories.blogspot.com

Constantina Alexander is a Tertiary Franciscan, a science tutor and an amateur astronomer with a lifelong interest in biblical stories. An accomplished iconographer, with commissioned work both in the UK and abroad, she now lives halfway up a mountain in Wales where she hopes to expand her creative repertoire for the glory of God.

Ruth Burgess is a member of the Iona Community living in Dunblane. She enjoys being retired, reading detective stories, writing and editing. Her garden is graced by a murder of crows and a shy wren.

Christopher was a school child in the East End of London in the 1970s. He was a fan of David Kossoff's Bible stories, which he listened to on schools radio.

Roddy Cowie is a retired Professor of Psychology, who specialised in emotion. He is now working on self-knowledge, and a Christian understanding of emotion. He is a lay reader in the Church of Ireland and an associate of the Iona Community.

Kathy Crawford is a Reader in the Diocese of Southwell & Nottingham. She lives in Gedling with her husband and two eldest grandchildren and is, in theory, retired!

Tricia Creamer is an associate of the Iona Community and a member of Poole Methodists, where she runs a weekly 'Celtic Colours' group exploring Christian spirituality through Celtic arts. She loves writing, teaching the piano and being involved with projects which bring people together.

Liz Crumlish is a Church of Scotland minister working on Renewal. She is a Board member of RevGalBlogPals, an international supportive community for women in ministry.

Liz Delafield is a Primary school teacher. She lives in Stockport, Greater Manchester with her husband Stewart and children Jennifer and Robert.

Judy Dinnen is a priest and poet and loves travelling. She served for three months in a Lutheran church in Bavaria last year. She appreciated the welcome she received, as well as the hospitality shown to refugees from around the world.

Brian Ford: 'I am a retired biology teacher. As well as writing Christian poetry I also write, and act in, pantomimes, and act in amateur productions of Shakespeare.'

Andrew Foster is an engineer living in Canada, an associate member of the Iona Community, an elder in the Presbyterian Church and a frequent visitor to Iona.

Pam Hathorn: 'I am a retired teacher who enjoys reading, especially poetry and Celtic prayers, and loves the night sky and the stars.'

Jo Love is a Resource Worker with the Wild Goose Resource Group. Her passions include long solitary walks, playing with art and words, and conversations that reach places beyond your usual after-church coffee. Her dream dinner guest would be Ecclesiastes.

Rebeka Maples is Director of Spiritual Formation for a programme to certify local pastors in the United Methodist Church. She retired from parish ministry after serving churches in the UK and US. She is a member of Spiritual Directors International and an associate member of the Iona Community.

Jane McBride is from Northern Ireland and has lived in Belgium for over 20 years. She works as a conference interpreter, is married, with three children, and is studying for a Research Masters in Theology at the University of Leuven.

Carolyn Morris: 'A long-time teacher and recently retired book creator and author, I am hoping to remain creative whilst coping with life-changing experiences.'

Jim Munro: 'My working life was spent teaching French at the Universities of Leeds and Stirling. I am currently a member of Alva Parish Church of Scotland.'

John Murning has worked in offices and industry and been a parish minister for 30 years, currently at Sherwood Greenlaw Church in Paisley. He is married to Linda and has two children.

Benjamin Pratt is a United Methodist minister who worked for many years as a pastoral counsellor. He is an advocate for caregivers and an author. His books include *A Guide for Caregivers* and *Short Stuff from the Tall Guy: Lenten Meditations on Seeking Peace in a Troubled World* (Read the Spirit). Benjamin lives near Washington DC with his wife, Judith.

John Randall: 'I have lived on Dartmoor for more than forty years. My relationship with the minor prophets goes back further still. Their anger at injustice has joined with what I have seen in Palestinians in their refusal to be either enemy or victim.'

Julie Rennick is a Church of Scotland minister serving in a country parish in the Scottish Borders. Her inspiration often comes when dog-walking in the hills and valleys that surround her.

Robert Shooter: 'Since retiring from social work and hospital chaplaincy I have put my time to walking, writing, reading and music.'

Thom M Shuman is retired into transitional ministry, and continues the daily discipline of writing. He enjoys reading, silence, his family – and really misses Scotland!

Spill the Beans is 'a lectionary-based resource with a Scottish flavour for Sunday Schools, Junior Churches and worship leaders': http://spillbeans.org.uk

Colin Taylor: 'I have learnt to rest in God's love, even when life proves a murky and unpleasant experience, because His love is always accessible, always abundant. I have needed His plenteous grace many times over the years, not least when ill health forced me to relinquish being a Church of England Reader. Although that avenue is closed, He still calls me, saying "Write the Vision" and He has truly given me lots to share.'

Kira Taylor: 'I'm a journalism student, passionate about social justice and equality.'

Simon Taylor is a Baptist minister and chaplain living and working in Exeter, Devon. He bakes bread on his days off.

Trevor Thorn is a lay minister in the Diocese of Ely who has a passion for encouraging the understanding that faith and science are complementary paths to perceiving the glory of God in his amazing universe. He publishes regularly on his poetry-based blog 'The Cross and The Cosmos': http://crossandcosmos.blogspot.com

Joy Tobler worked for most of her adult life in a Bible translation ministry in both Brazil and the UK.

Liz Varley, after a long and varied life in ministry, is now a novice with the Society of the Sisters of Bethany. Our work is to pray for the unity of all Christians and to give hospitality in Jesus' name.

Marjory J.B. Williamson, a retired Chartered Accountant and an elder at Abronhill Parish Church in Cumbernauld, has been interested in creative worship since her Youth Fellowship days. She is a Trustee of the Church Hymnary Trust and of ALTERnativity.

Index of authors

Wild Goose Publications is part of the Iona Community:

- An ecumenical movement of men and women from different walks of life and different traditions in the Christian church
- Committed to the gospel of Jesus Christ, and to following where that leads, even into the unknown
- Engaged together, and with people of goodwill across the world, in acting, reflecting and praying for justice, peace and the integrity of creation
- Convinced that the inclusive community it seeks must be embodied in the community it practises

Together with its staff, the community is responsible for:

- The islands residential centres of Iona Abbey, the MacLeod Centre on Iona, and Camas Adventure Centre on the Ross of Mull

and in Glasgow:

- The administration of the Community
- Work with young people
- A publishing house, Wild Goose Publications
- Its association in the revitalising of worship with the Wild Goose Resource Group

The Iona Community was founded in Glasgow in 1938 by George MacLeod, minister, visionary and prophetic witness for peace, in the context of the poverty and despair of the Depression. Its original task of rebuilding the monastic ruins of Iona Abbey became a sign of hopeful rebuilding of community in Scotland and beyond. Today, it consists of about 280 Members, mostly in Britain, and 1500 Associate Members, with 1400 Friends worldwide. Together and apart, the community 'follows the light it has, and prays for more light'.

For information on the Iona Community contact:
The Iona Community, 21 Carlton Court, Glasgow G5 9JP, UK.
Phone: 0141 429 7281
e-mail: admin@iona.org.uk; web: www.iona.org.uk

For enquiries about visiting Iona, please contact:
Iona Abbey, Isle of Iona, Argyll PA76 6SN, UK.
Phone: 01681 700404
e-mail: enquiries@iona.org.uk

For books, CDs & digital downloads published by Wild Goose Publications: www.ionabooks.com

Wild Goose Publications, the publishing house of the Iona Community established in the Celtic Christian tradition of Saint Columba, produces books, e-books, CDs and digital downloads on:

- holistic spirituality
- social justice
- political and peace issues
- healing
- innovative approaches to worship
- song in worship, including the work of the Wild Goose Resource Group
- material for meditation and reflection

For more information:

Wild Goose Publications
21 Carlton Court,
Glasgow G5 9JP, UK

Tel. +44 (0)141 429 7281
e-mail: admin@ionabooks.com

or visit our website at
www.ionabooks.com
for details of all our products and online sales